INTRODUCING FEMINIST THEOLOGY

SECOND EDITION

INTRODUCING FEMINIST THEOLOGY
SECOND EDITION

Lisa Isherwood and
Dorothea McEwan

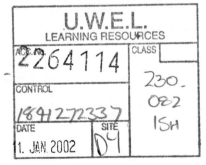

Sheffield
Academic Press
www.SheffieldAcademicPress.com

Second edition 2001

Copyright © 1993, 1994, 2001 Sheffield Academic Press

Published by Sheffield Academic Press Ltd
Mansion House
19 Kingfield Road
Sheffield S11 9AS
England

www.SheffieldAcademicPress.com

Printed on acid-free paper in Great Britain
by The Cromwell Press
Trowbridge, Wiltshire

British Library Cataloguing-in-Publication Data

A catalogue record for this book is available
from the British Library

ISBN 1-84127-233-7

Table of Contents

Preface to the Second Edition

This new edition of *Introducing Feminist Theology* shows the vibrancy and development of feminist theologies in the last few years. Not only have we witnessed that feminist tenets took root in societies and churches and lives lived individually, we also have experienced the growth of scholarship in theologies rooted in women's concerns and aspirations. We therefore felt the need to update this introductory guide to and through feminist theologies.

The insight and interpretations both of theory and fact are the fruits of reading and discussing, teaching and experimenting and most of all, of listening to women in their quest to bring their own understanding to a wider readership. The biggest shift in understanding in the last few years happened in the field of a monolithic block called 'feminist theology', but of a glorious diversity of 'feminist theologies'.

Thus this book is not a dictionary giving water-tight definitions, but a 'how to' tool for getting to grips with feminist theologies and setting out on one's own way of discovery.

The journey is the goal.

Dorothea and Lisa
October 2000

Introduction

Setting the Scene

Feminism is a way of looking at society and centring the concerns of society on women and men. Feminist theologies as contextual theologies are dealing with these experiences and concerns in the realm of everyday living, making connections to enhance the practical and ethical solutions, to connect individual to societal demands and to facilitate human endeavours to form relationships built on mutuality and to grow into a relationship with the divine. As such, feminist theologies, rooted as they are in a plethora of theologies of liberation, offer an analysis of theology, a critique of theory, thought patterns and of the praxis of religions and a model for doing theology in a transformative way. Feminism, arising out of the experiences of multi-layered oppressions, is about women refusing to be controlled by definitions of who and what they should be. As Christians we come from a misogynist tradition, the tradition of exclusion still rampant for instance in the RC Church. Our problem as women in the churches was the problem of relationship of structure and development. There it was, the almighty structure, meting out laws and rules and woe to those who broke them. And at the same time there was resistance, non-conformism, dissent, the healthy attitude of posing questions: why do those in power, the structure, want me to behave in a particular way, when my own experience tells me that I am right and you are wrong?

The *ekklesia*, the community, founded by Jesus Christ, called to end discrimination between women and men, slaves and free, foes and friends (Gal. 3.28), has in its long history become an instrument of exclusion for half of its members. (Many contemporary readings of Gal. 3 suggest this should not be a surprise since Paul was looking for the restoration of the original glorious creation in all its unitary splendour—woman would disappear in this eschatological harmony.) The offices of deacons, priests and bishops are closed to women in many Christian churches and are in the RC church narrowly maintained by men, celibate men. The clerical upper caste denies women access to and exercise of the ordained offices on the basis of one-sided interpretations of 'tradition', 'authority' and gospel teachings. These, in fact, only show the whole breadth of sociological, pyschological and anthropological arguments of fear, cementing the very discriminations that Jesus Christ wanted to dismantle.

The vision of equality and entitlement has become caught in rhetoric. Today, women and men want to take part in decision making. They want to safeguard rights and to control their own lives. In the social and political arena this has led to wider social movement, in the theological arena to the emergence of liberation theology, in the Latin American context, that is the fundamental idea that the poor can do theology can engage in theological reflections which issues in the radical process of participation. They have learnt and understood that personal life decisions cannot be left to outsiders or defined by experts, be they religious, educational, professional and so on. In fact, if decisions are left to 'experts' the opposite happens: decisions become harmful when the ideas and visions of the people themselves are termed wrong, and the 'right' decisions are imposed on them from outside. The text, the gospel, is important, but also the context, the field in which it is sited, lived and taught. And once people understood that decisions taken elsewhere, by an outside command centre, somewhere outside their context, were harmful, were not meeting their local needs, these same people realized that their spiritual needs were no longer met through existing structures.

However, while the liberation theologians were acutely aware of the injustices done to the people in their care, they did not see that a similar set of injustices were perpetrated by state and church against women. Out of this realization feminist theology was born.

> In order to get a grip on our topic, we need to prepare our tools, we need to define feminism and feminist theology. 'Feminism sees patriarchy as a multi-layered system of domination, centered in men's control of women, but including class, race, and generational hierarchies, clericalism, war, and the domination of nature' (Ruether 1997: 4).

Feminism, thus, is an analysis of society from a woman's point of view, the radical notion that women are people and not animals, legal minors, beasts of burden. Feminist theology defines women and men as created equal and 'denounces male domination of women as sin' (Ruether 1997: 3). The task of dismantling the patterns of patriarchal Christianity is to reconstruct a radically different understanding of the key teachings (God, humanity, male and female, sin and fall, Christ and redemption).

Christian feminists of both sexes are working to root religious experience in the here and now and to place theological insights in the here and now. If one believes in the message of salvation, the faith message of Christianity, then feminism offers a critique of contemporary patriarchal and kyriarchal theology. The task for the hierarchy is not that it is asked to share power, but that it is asked to change its views. It can do so and, in fact, has done so over the centuries. Here are just three examples from history when church-as-structure saw the necessity to change its views and to move with the faithful, with the times, with the needs of ordinary people: (1) the abolition of slavery. Until the nineteenth century the churches believed that slavery was a god-given state in society; only reluctantly, in the wake of civil legislation, did they accept a shift in thinking; (2) the enthronement of every new pope in the Middle Ages. The elders of the Jewish community in Rome had to present him with the Torah, which, being identical with the Pentateuch, he acknowledged with the words 'We confirm the Law, but we condemn your faith and your interpretation' *(confirmamus sed non consentimus)*'. The ceremony occurred for the first time in 1119 and was last performed under Leo X in 1513. In later years it was transferred indoors to shield the Jewish delegates from ill-treatment by the crowd (Gregorovius 1923: 286-87); (3) it took the RC Church until November 1992 to declare that Galileo, the great Italian mathematician, who died in 1642, was right and the church was wrong: the earth is not flat, it is, in fact, round. By pointing out these facts, we do show that there is development of argument, although painfully slow in some churches.[1]

If the churches as institutions cannot reform themselves and move with the times, they may, in fact, cease to provide spiritual leadership and be left behind while people for whom church life is important, 'the church as people', will move on, leaving the old wineskins behind, much as Christianity left Judaism behind.

---

1. The following topics were once condemned by the RC Church, but are no longer condemned: freedom of conscience, democracy, demanding interest on loans, bible study, mass in the vernacular language, worshipping with non-Catholics, the crucifix as blasphemous. And topics which were once accepted by the RC Church but are no longer so: all sexual desire is sinful, torture and burning of heretics, persecution of Jews, married priests, women priests, slavery, the sun revolving round the earth.

Feminist theologies supply the tools to make the shift from seeing religion as controlling life or the world to seeing religion as valuing the contribution of each and everyone. Feminism is not about making the world woman-centred, but about bringing the world into balance, offering a way out of age-old dualisms and discrimination to inclusion and mutuality.

'Tradition', the handing over of tales, beliefs, practices, is a healthy way of incorporating the wisdom of our foremothers into our experiences. It becomes unhealthy when the past is only allowed to live on in one-sided presentations of the past, called 'truth', and the present with all its flux and flow is deemed to be disruptive of that which is termed truth. But truth cannot be escaped from. Historic facts will come to light, they are facets of the picture that we have to strive to complete. Gustav Mahler famously spoke up against a slavish adherence to tradition by coining the phrase 'tradition is not the worship of the ashes, but keeping the fire alive'.[2] The history of resistance, of dissent, of thinking for oneself is as old as the history of the Christian churches. However, it was swept under the carpet or, to use a modern word, marginalized, and those who insisted on it were declared heretics, confused, even Godless, heathens, members of sects. Here we do not have the space to examine the history of discrimination perpetuated by the churches. We have to make do with simple shorthand expressions; suffice it to say that church history was written by the winners. Men, women and children were slaughtered in the Crusades in the twelfth and thirteenth centuries, mostly women were persecuted and burnt in the witch craze in the sixteenth and seventeenth centuries, Protestants were expelled from their homesteads in the seventeenth and eighteenth centuries and were 'allowed' to emigrate and Jews were annihilated in the wake of anti-judaist and anti-semitic pogroms in the nineteenth and twentieth centuries. The history of the Christian churches is also a history in the name of persecution of people who were termed outsiders, others, foes. The mechanism of exclusion is still extant against homosexuals and lesbians who are taught to live in a particular way and in general against women who are told they are not material for priesthood in some churches. Those who do not conform have to reckon with punishment. But thanks to the insistence, the stubborn attitude of many women and men borne of experience there is development, even if painfully slow.

2.   Translation by Dorothea McEwan.

The Steps of Discernment

Feminist theologies, first expressed by scholars coming from a Christian background, but then taken on by scholars from a variety of theological backgrounds, proceed with their analyses in three steps:

1. They critique the standard accounts of faith and practice, the dicta of the church fathers and religious writers, the treatment of ethical issues *inter alia*.

2. They scrutinize writings on theology, history, doctrine, scriptures to find the sources of oppression, the presumptions and assumptions, the faulty interpretations that dictate what women are and are not allowed to do and what is pleasing to a God referred to as father. The one-sided views perpetrated by a theology of complementarity of the sexes, one complementing the other, neither sex being whole on its own account, are still put forward in the Christian tradition, for example by the Holy See, as the way to rule the relations between the sexes. This very view makes a mockery of the rule of celibate priesthood, because the theology of complementarity means that celibate male priests by not being allowed to experience complementarity with the female sex, do not have the whole span of experiences in their relationships with others.

3. They search in the same sources for the liberating strands that have been obscured, even redacted out, in the Christian tradition; for example, the actions of Jesus consorting with a variety of people, women, as a matter of course, among them.

The critique, the search for the limits and the search for the liberation shows the scope for feminist theological scholarship. It peels away the notions of inferiority of women, of differentiations as a value system. New groups emerge, stressing the importance of relationships, of justice making, of locating truths in the lived experience, of the need for solidarity. Thus, it is not so much religious tenets that are seen as problematical, or not all the time, but one-sided interpretations of them, particularly when male religious leaders blot out women's views and experiences, make women's experiences invisible, their role only complementary and deny them their function as religious agents.

Christianity has a vision of making living together possible, interacting on a personal and societal level beyond classism, racism and sexism. But

measured against the history of the last 2000 years, this vision has spec-
tacularly failed to be put into practice. We still see institutionalized sexism, sexist structures in churches and states. How can we deal with this
scenario? How can half a theology be turned into a whole one? Women
belong to churches that say they follow the example of Jesus, but have
institutionalized sexism. How can women keep their integrity as individuals, endowed with God-given talents and charisms, when they understand that in order to follow the example of Jesus they have to break
with these structures? Nowhere else in society do women concur with
their own oppression willingly. Duty, fashion and sex are examples, but
women are not compelled to accept them, whereas in religion women
are compelled to accept second-rate status.

These are practical questions and points, based on the fundamental
consideration: how do we shape or mould experiences into theologies?
Patriarchal theologies, undergirded by a trinity expressed in male gender
constructs, erect universal systems into which to fit individuals. This has
borne disastrous fruits, with attempts to force human behaviour into one
mould and human behaviour not fitting into this one mould declared as
sick, deviating, faulty. One example is, of course, the treatment of
homosexuality; another is the misogyny perpetrated by the churches,
based on a faulty understanding of physiology, which thereby produces a
theology flawed to the core. Aquinas's view, based on Aristotle, of
women as misbegotten males springs to mind (*ST* I, 99, 2, and 1).

Feminist theologies are attempts to start with the individual and to
stay with individual experience while also creating networks and communities of mutual empowerment. These communities are imaged as
taking the experiences of individuals and building on them, valuing
them, they conceptualize a framework that builds up and not one that
limits or eliminates experiences. Thus feminist thinkers have stressed that
they do not build systems, structures or hierarchies; instead, they have
emphasized the values of networking. As contextual theologies feminist
theologies hold many a mirror to patriarchal societies and churches.
What the mirrors show is the exclusion of women from public culture,
an androcentric bias of all public culture and an asymmetrical relationship between men and women, very often even understood as God-
given. Therefore the leading spiritual feminists, Rosemary Radford
Ruether, Mary Hunt, Elisabeth Schüssler Fiorenza, Letty Russell in the
US, Daphne Hampson, Mary Grey, Grace Jantzen in the UK, to name
but a few, summarize the goal of feminist theologies as the

transformation of patriarchal theologies. These theologies might at long last catch up with developments in those societies in which women and men share equal rights.

In this introduction we want to highlight that feminist theologies are praxis-based ways of doing theology, based on the individual experiences of women and men. Theology has always based its codes on lived experiences. Feminist theologies as contextual theologies locate the experiences of women as a source for doing theology. Theology used to be done from the neck up—and the white collar worn by priests still indicates the separating line between thinking and feeling. Spiritual feminists want to include the whole body in the process of theologizing. The very understanding that theologies no longer can coerce women into accepting views damaging to women started the threefold analysis of critique, the search for the limits and the search for the liberation from the limits.

The Critique

The first task was to unravel a package of misogynist assumptions and patriarchal presumptions that woman were sexually attractive but morally abhorrent, which flowed into church laws, scripture interpretations, explanations of theologies and cosmologies. So powerful were these sexist views that they took root not only in churches governing societal concerns but also in state legislation. It took courageous thinkers and campaigners from the seventeeth century onward to start the process of separating church from state, a process we call today the Enlightenment shift. Fundamental change came from replacing the public notions of religion as state religion by a personal understanding of religion. It is important here not to confuse personal understanding with privatized notions of religion. Privatized notions issue into pious lifestyles without concerns for societal dimensions of faith, whereas personal notions flow into communal actions, societal awareness, the justice-making agenda that rejects the 'power over' model of authoritarian religions in favour of a 'power for' model of religious insights of relationality.

One very important part of this change was the research into the history of women's exclusion and the justifications put forward for this exclusion by the hierarchical establishments. In all congregations in all Christian churches women are in the majority; statistics show that the percentage is consistently between 60 and 71 per cent. There is some evidence that this has been the case throughout history. Christianity rose through the social classes primarily through women, slaves, freed women, middle- and upper-class women, brides who converted their bridegrooms, mothers who converted their sons. The Christian churches did not break the societal pattern of male supremacy in public life, but accepted it within its administration. The direct result was that women were excluded from official leadership; the fierce polemic in the Greek Bible against leadership only testifies to a power struggle that the women lost. What followed was the rhetoric of oppression: women have to be silent in church; consequent upon this followed the practice of oppression: women have to be controlled. Why? They are the more irrational, spirit-filled people, given to witchcraft, unreliable, and so on were the stereotypes quickly put forward. I remember being told in school why women cannot be priests: because they could not keep secret information received in confession, their conduct would be unreliable, they were unsuitable for leadership roles. Whether confession was such a good thing never entered into the discussion.

The argument of tradition, that there was always male leadership in the Christian churches, is the argument based on the tradition of exclusion. Yet, underneath this tradition, older than this notion, is the vision of Christianity as a radically egalitarian way of life. It is this vision that guides feminist theologians in their work, supplying an ethical grounding by understanding these scriptural affirmations as justice-making, dependent on individual circumstances, on the reality of individuation and relationality and not dependent on discriminatory assumptions.

For the first time it is women who are leaving the mainstream churches. At the same time it is women who are hungry for theology, wanting to find out the rules and regulations that stamp them with being second-class citizens, which credit them with having 'brought sin into the world' and similar ill-informed views and rhetoric. Once you start reading scriptures and rule books from a point of view of researching why churches and societies have such a dismal record on women, you will see how much they are based on gross stereotyping, such as woman the temptress; on faulty physiology, such as man the norm and woman the deviation of norm; on arrogant assumptions, that women are in need of punishment and control. Moreover, you will realize how many layers of contempt have been incapacitating women in churches and societies, safeguarding and upholding the view that churches arrogate to themselves the position of guardians of morality.

The binary model of the 'good' woman, housewife, mother, nurturer and nurse and secondly, the 'bad' woman, temptress, whore and witch, has done immeasurable damage to societies and churches everywhere in Europe and beyond throughout the centuries. Woman became an object, her radius of action became firmly circumscribed, her work went largely unremunerated. For centuries little or no education meant that women had no power of collaborating with men on an equal footing in church and society.

The last hundred years have seen a great change, a development, a flowering of opportunities, taken by women as well as created by women to bring their vision, their understanding of cooperation and non-confrontation out of the spinning rooms of their homes into the mainstream life of their communities. The work for the abolition of slavery was vigorously forwarded by women in the US, the work for the suffrage of women was courageously undertaken by women in many countries in Europe. A wide range of educational opportunities led to a variety of professional work where women became accepted as equal.

Researching the Sources of Oppression

A discourse that is serious about finding a way to include all people in a given worship community and to put into practice tenets of inclusivity in churches, worship communities, societies, organizations, is a hallmark of a new way of doing theology. This new way is not so new any longer. Process thought from the 1930s onward and liberation theologies from the 1960s onward led in time to findings that proved important for the development of feminist theologies.

Feminism, an analysis of societies from a woman's point of view, and theologies, reflections upon the nature of the deity and its implications on societies, impacted on each other and produced a debate on religion and spirituality; on the place of women and men in creation; on the power structures between those who are marginalized and those who marginalize; on the political outflow of religious prescriptions on societies—to name just a few. Over the past 30 years an enormous body of writing, teaching and practical application has sprung up around the world, exploring different ways of interaction. The hallmarks of these explorations were and are emphasis on experience, mutuality, creativity, relationality, respect, nurture and a new understanding of equality. Thus, feminism and theologies anchored in an understanding that values everybody and not just one group of humankind have produced feminist theologies that to many women and men are invigorating, energizing and life-loving or 'biophilic', to speak with Mary Daly (Daly and Caputi 1988: 67).

Today we witness a strange dichotomy of equality in civil law (where formal equality as enshrined in democratic laws has developed further into substantive equality in societies), but inequality in church laws: While in societies at large women have gained access to work, the situation in the churches is quite different. While in some denominations women can now train to become ministers and priests, other denominations still refuse women any sacramental and managerial position, and equality of the sexes in the churches is still not achieved in the majority of them. The equality discussion, however, cannot be tackled only from a societal point of view. It must be tackled from a theological point of view as well. The traditional view in the Christian churches used to be that women were presumed to be unequal and fundamentally inferior in nature, but as baptized Christians this disability was washed away. However, in the last 200 years a switch has taken place and today we can no longer talk of women's inequality in nature. Societal experiences simply do not subscribe to such an interpretation any longer, so in order to justify the continued exclusion of women from ministry, modern Catholic teaching now accepts women as 'equal' in nature, namely secular society, 'but unequal in grace'. The creational image-of-God interpretation includes women, whereas the image-of-Christ interpretation, as put forward in the discussion on ministry, excludes women. The theological packaging is still the reason for women's exclusion from formal ministry and priesthood in the RC Church (Ruether 1991: 11-18).

This is just one example of one church's sexism and just one example of how the 'nature-of-women' discussion excludes women. This discussion produces many justifications for stereotyping women, for telling women what to do and what not to do. While churches take a stand against exploitation and abuse on a wide range of issues, they do not unequivocally adopt the same stand when it comes to women in their own employment or when it comes to fighting—in solidarity with women—to stop abuse and exploitation as and when they occur in societies and churches.

The power of naming is a topic well researched in feminist theologies. The way language is used tells a great deal about unspoken assumptions in a given cultural context. Religious language was for centuries an example of exclusive language in which 'man' was the norm for humanity, 'woman' was the deviation from the norm. The search for inclusive language went hand in hand with feminist theologies. Experiments with new ways of using old words excited many people and sparked a burst of creativity for alternative service books, new translations of the Bible, new hymns and so on. Old linguistic boundaries were questioned. Exclusive definitions of words were abandoned, words were reclaimed and claimed for inclusive use. An example of this development is the use of the word 'synod'. A meeting of bishops, as a dictionary would explain, was, until a very short time ago, a meeting of men, laying down the law for men and women in their spiritual care. By returning to the original meaning of the word 'synod' as 'coming together', 'meeting', a signal was given that issued in the creation of women's synods.

New Sources. The Process of Metanoia

The technical term 'Enlightenment shift', the understanding that the individual determines the structure, and not vice versa, that happened in Europe in the seventeenth and eighteenth centuries and that freed the human mind from psychological obstacles, in time triggered developments in societies and churches. Vital developments by women in religion are characteristic of late twentieth-century life. Women posed questions, women centred their concerns not only on small segments of their society, but on all of society, women established the notion of feminism, that radical notion, that women share full humanity with men. This notion, first, the awareness of women's oppression and exploitation in society, at work and within the family, decreed by the churches, and secondly, the conscious action by women and men to change this situation,

> developed the thinking of personhood, of personal value, of the value of personal experience. Not those in authority can and should dictate to others, but authority has to be opened up, has to be newly defined as empowerment, taking power for oneself. Not any longer a dictate to love authority, but to love with authority (McEwan 1994: 41-48).

This ushered in a fundamental change 'in understanding replacing the privatized notion of religion with a communal one, rejecting the "power over" model in favor of letting people be religious in a variety of ways, and rejoicing in the fact that religious traditions are made up of sisters and brothers who share equally and uniquely in the development of their content' (Hunt 1989: 85).

Through this enlightenment shift, societies have become more open, more democratic or contributive and accountable. This became a challenge to the churches, some of which have accepted this shift although some still ignore it. In those ignoring traditions believers were and are told that the church is the expression of God's will, that the theology is fixed and new insights cannot be gained. Women experience God's call, but the church does not allow women to answer the call. Women bake the bread, but cannot break the bread; full access to the priesthood is denied to women simply because of their biological gender.

The importance of the concept of 'counter-tradition', not so much as a different 'tradition', but as an expansion of tradition, has opened up the fertile field of women's studies analysing the intellectual input of women towards liberation. In France, Olympe de Gouges published her declaration of the rights of women *Déclaration des droits de la femme et de la citoyenne* in 1791, in England Mary Wollstonecraft wrote her influential book on the rights of women *A Vindication of the Rights of Woman* in 1792 (and incidentally Theodor Gottlieb von Hippel wrote on the improvement for women in the same year, *Über die bürgerliche Verbesserung der Weiber*). Proto-feminists and early feminists in the UK and the US drew on their Christian tradition and a radical notion of equality that fed into their feminisms. In the US the women's movement was born out of the abolition movement. Women fought to participate in the abolitionist campaigns of the 1830s, fighting to win the right to speak in public against slavery. Sarah Grimké and her sister Angelina were among the first who spoke out that discriminatory legislation against non-Whites was on a par with discriminatory legislation against women. The abolitionist Sojourner Truth and her rallying cry 'And ain't I a woman?' (29 May 1851) electrified her audience. In the 1890s Elizabeth Cady Stanton and a group of friends published *The Woman's Bible*, attacking the male bias of the Greek Bible, excising passages that were misogynist. It was a radical way of dealing with a text that had, in their eyes, damaged women over the centuries.[3] The Young Women's Christian Association, the Woman's Christian Temperance Union in the US, the Protestant 'Social Gospel' movement in Canada, atttracted many members. Thus, notions of social justice and social reform

---

3. Cullen Murphy's book *The Word According to Eve* (Harmondsworth: Penguin, 2000) is a present-day investigation on a similar line.

informed notions of justice in the churches, notably the new movements
for the ordination of women to the ministerial priesthood. Campaigners
like Dorothy Day in the US, the founder of the Catholic Worker
Movement in the 1930s, and women orders starting out on social work,
radicalized the women's movement.

The different social settings of the establishment and university system
of countries in Europe after World War II meant that women could
start to get an education in theology at university level. Women gradu-
ates started to write theology and inspire new generations of theology
students. Topics ranged from civil liberties to equal pay, woman-friendly
and family-friendly legislation in the labour market, to an end of loss of
property rights in marriage and inequitable divorce and child custody
laws, an end to exploitation of women, demands for an end of discrimination of women in churches, feminist hermeneutics, feminist biblical
scholarship and epistemology. Nelle Morton became the first woman in
the US to teach a university course on women, theology and language
at Drew University, Madison, New Jersey, and wrote about it years later
in *The Journey is Home* (Boston: Beacon Press, 1985). Valerie Saiving,
US theology student, published the article 'The Human Situation: A
Feminine View' in 1960 in which she spelt out that she was a student of
theology as well as a woman; her article was to become a watershed.[4]
Her particular insight was that the human condition, as discussed by
theological writers, left out the experience of women and did not
understand that there were cognitive differences in posing questions that
would result in different answers. In the spring of 1970 Rosemary
Radford Ruether at Yale expounded the theory of the interrelationship
of sexism and dualism (Stuckey 1998). Phyllis Trible became an out-
standing Hebrew Bible scholar, who, in 1973, discussed women's liberation and the Hebrew Scriptures in 'Women in the Old Testament'
(Trible 1973). In quick succession scholars like Mary Daly, Elisabeth
Schüssler Fiorenza, Rosemary Radford Ruether, Beverley Wildung
Harrison, Daphne Hampson and Letty M. Russell searched and researched scriptures and church documents, and scoured archives for new
sources on women's histories. Feminist scholarship was flowering and
was building up a critical mass of scholarship which, in turn, opened up
university courses on feminism, feminist theology, Christian feminism,
feminist theory around the world, Mercy Amba Oduyoye (Nigeria),
Elizabeth Amoah (Ghana), Marie Assad (Egypt), Bette Ekeya (Kenya),

---

4.   *The Journal of Religion* (1960), republished in Christ and Plaskow 1979: 25-42.

Louise Tappa (Cameroon), Aruna Gnanadason (India), Marianne Katoppo (Indonesia), Chung Hyun Kyung (Korea), to name but a few (Isherwood and McEwan 1996).

While some influential scholars like Rosemary Radford Ruether wrote and write from a position within their church, others like Mary Daly have left their former church affiliation behind and have become an icon for women who can no longer accept the continued discrimination in their churches. The established churches do nothing spiritually for them. They are like the early modern dissenters and non-conformists who, practicing local democracy, put themselves outside the dominant parish/administrative system.

Today the situation is highlighted by a rise in fundamentalisms, across the world and across the major religions. Fundamentalisms concentrate on women as, in some societies, the moral rectitude of a given social group is measured by the obedience of women. This is a new threat or rather, the old limitations dressed up in new garb: religious traditions have devalued women, new, fundamentalist traditions, continue betraying women by prescribing strict guidelines on morality. We are faced with reconfiguring history, going away from the eschatological scenario only, the apocalypticism of doom-mongers with their notions of inevitable tribulations and find access to life-giving, biophilic ways of thinking and living.

The Challenges Ahead

Women who are spiritual feminists are faced with a problem: How can they be active in a transformative way in their churches and denominations and theologies, when they do not have equal rights? The answer has to be that theologies touch women and men and the community of women and men needs inclusive models for doing theology, not the dichotomy of ordained and non-ordained, a hierarchically stratified model.

Every form of religion has degraded women. So-called societal norms quoted religious ideas to underpin a variety of measures that were actually harmful to women: in China the practice of footbinding; in India the practice of suttee (the burning of widows on the funeral pyres of their husbands); in some Islamic countries genital mutilation; in Judaism and Christianity a stifling of creativity because the faith systems tell women who and what they are, notably that they are second-class, sinful and seductive, and need to be 'kept' by men. The fact is that sexism, a stereotyping because of sex, 'is part of the intricate web of oppression in which most of us live, and that having attuned ourselves to it does not make it any less a fact of oppression' (Fabella 1983: 249, quoting Oduyoye speaking at the 5th International Conference of the Ecumenical Association Third World Theologians in New Delhi, 1981) or, to speak in the words of Ivan Illich, 'a hitherto unthinkable individual degradation of one half of humanity on socio-biological grounds' (Illich 1983: 34).

What, then, do women and men, interested in equality, equity, liberation and feminist values, aim for? Their visions and hopes can be loosely grouped into three areas:

(1) Women and men want the social teaching of the churches, the 'Love your neighbour' command, radically enacted, going to the roots, taken up and lived. We see it in the base communities in Latin America and in experimental worship groups in Great Britain and in many other countries.

(2) Women and men use imaginative methods to change their way of participation, their status as religious agents, their understanding of doing theology and being church. It might be language, which is inclusive, it might be action, which is inclusive in the life of the community, it might be a lifestyle.

(3) Women and men want to put the history and tradition of misogyny behind them. When the bishops quote the tradition of the RC Church of not having women priests, they only refer to a tradition of exclusion and woman-hatred, of hurt being done to women, which is a-Christian to the core and the sooner we put it behind us the better. For, if we look closely at 'tradition', we know that a number of shifts have occurred. We have to ask the bishops what they mean by 'tradition'.

Christianity has a vision of making living together possible, the loving pursuit of making right relationships, interacting on a personal and societal level beyond classism, racism and sexism. This is the agenda for the present. We believe as women we can help the churches to develop and we believe that we as women can contribute to this vision.

PART I

Chapter 1

Man as Norm

'The Woman problem has always been a man's problem'

Why has Western culture developed the view that man is the norm? Simone de Beauvoir, quoting J.-P. Sartre, says 'Anti-semitism is not a Jewish problem; it is our problem' and concludes correctly that 'the woman problem has always been a man's problem' (1988: 159). It has too often been the case that the oppressed, 'the victim', has been held responsible by the oppressor, the perpetrator of the crime. In this way responsibility has been shifted, and so, by implication, has the obligation to solve the problem. 'It is your fault for being Jewish, for being female' —at this point patriarchal logic takes over. The rest is history. Sadly, it is the history of prejudice, exploitation, hate and injustice. Such history only becomes possible by operating with categories of opposing dualisms; this is exactly what patriarchy has done and why feminism finds it destructive. By looking at the development of Western culture, we start a twofold process of investigating the emergence of 'norm' and the emergence of male as norm.

Politics and religion both work in society and each share collective responsibility for the individual. Politics, with its emphasis on borders and laws and military power, is concerned with transmitting rights and defending rights. The Christian community is founded on the concept of all-encompassing love and forgiveness. However, when it became enmeshed in a political system and more so, when it became a state religion following the conversion of the Roman emperor Constantine the Great, it absorbed into its structure political concepts that ran counter to Christian ideals. In time, the religion of love and forgiveness sanctioned institutionalized racism, classism and sexism.

To trace the historical development of racism, sexism and classism in Christianity is an important task. However, we can only acknowledge here the fact that discrimination on the grounds of race, sex and class was and is a reality within Christian history: for example, until the nineteenth century slavery was accepted as God-given, sexism was seen in the exclusion of women from decision-making processes in the church going back to the second century and classism was perpetuated by the church through notions of nobility, clergy and laity. The religious response to this situation can be measured next to the secular response. In the secular sphere in the wake of the Enlightenment and nineteenth-century liberal thinking, the process of dismantling discrimination built on racist, sexist and classist prejudices was started. Following the lead of humanitarian politicians the churches eventually acknowledged that slavery was an evil and that racism was an evil. We could hardly claim that racism has been eradicated but at least it is faced as a problem. But churches still have a long way to go to eradicate sexism and classism in their own institutions and to promote their eradication in society as a whole.

Sociologists tell us that it is the function of the third generation to dig up what the second generation tried hard to forget about the first generation. For third generation, in this context, read present day Christian feminists, for second generation the rather bloated church regiment from Constantine to Vatican II, some 1600 years of patriarchy, and for first generation read the apostolic churches and their development.

In the wake of a whole range of feminist scholarship what we as the third generation are busily digging up, literally resurrecting, is the true character of the Christian church, as instituted by Christ, led and shepherded in diverse settings by people with diverse gifts, male and female, Gentile and Jew, slave and free. We do so in order to highlight where the second generation went wrong, after being freed from the disabilities of being an underground movement, by setting up an oppressive structure. We set out to look at the sources, at their interpretation throughout history and at the discussion of contemporary women's experiences. We do so from our perspective, the perspective of oppression and conditioning that clashes harshly with the mission of the church of bringing the good news.

A wealth of books has been written, research conducted, courses given in which hierarchical prescriptions have been analysed and found wanting and in which sexist prohibitions have been unmasked (e.g. Dale Spender, Ann Oakley, Simone de Beauvoir, Mary Wollstonecraft among many others). In our time, traditional theology lags behind developments in society. Ideas about God, the nature of God, the person of Mary, the creation of the world, the praxis of faith, to name but a few, are enshrined in doctrines that no longer express the consensus of the faithful. The churches can no longer insist that believers adhere to doctrines that go against the experiences of the believers. No longer can it claim to uphold these once accepted opinions unchanged in societies that are quite different from the ones in which these rules originated.

Feminism and feminist theology want to engage in a critique of traditional politics and theology in order to trigger a process of investigation, rethink, change and ultimate transformation within patriarchal society and religious institutions. Change will hurt; it always does. Think of the pains Chinese women suffered in the first half of this century once they started unbinding their crippled feet, tiny, lifeless, dysfunctional limbs, which originally had been bound up to conform to and to produce an ideal of 'beauty', but in reality to stop them from running away from their male master. Change does hurt, but the many women who have been through it bear witness to other women and men that change and growth are not only possible, but creative. Christianity is not about being lame, but about being a pilgrim. As an incarnational and resurrection faith, it gives hope that even death can be transformed and so the death of patriarchy need not be seen as the end but rather as a new beginning.

Where Do We Start?

In the 1970s the British government published a booklet entitled 'Protect and Survive', a guide about surviving a nuclear attack. Those who found the measures advocated inadequate, published another booklet called 'Protest and Survive'. In it they queried the whole policy of nuclear weapons. We believe that the operative word in this debate was 'protest'. We meet here two diametrically opposed sets of ideas: one set has to do with protecting the integrity of tradition; the other is to do with protesting against a tradition that has turned out to be abusive. We want to offer to a dysfunctional church and society a faith that stresses the importance of right relationships.

Democracy means taking part, participating in the decision-making process, having an opinion, speaking out and if need be, protesting. Women have been marginalized in church and society. However, the process of democratization in society has allowed women at long last equal access to participation; in the Roman Catholic and Orthodox churches this is still resisted. Surely a hierarchical view can no longer be tolerated when our understanding of society is based on the value of the individual and not on the value of the 'ruling class', in this case the clergy. Women on the margin of the church assume the role of prophets. They protest against the injustices emanating from the pinnacle, because from their position outside the power arena, they see how inequalities affect those on the margin—and in the ultimate analysis those at the pinnacle as well. They have nothing to protect because participation as equals is denied them. To protest is a way to survive. To protest is the way to deal with the situation, forcefully, but non-violently, peacefully, to enter into dialogue and to learn to understand phobias and fears. As women we have the example of the Suffragettes, who protested, non-violently in the political arena for women's rights. These women with their peaceful, persistent protest changed the course of history.

So What Do they Say of Us?

Woman is a wonderful piece of the furniture of fancy. Traditionalist men, when called to defend their position, reason along the lines: 'It brings out the best points in a man if he is made to feel that he is master of the situation'.[1] Such a statement is based on an understanding of woman as childlike and in need of protection. It is almost a throw-back to the myth of man the hunter, who engages in dangerous pursuits while 'his woman' remains secure at home. If danger threatens the home, he is there to defend his rights and his property, which includes his wife. Women have had to play along and see themselves in the role of the object, the object of protection, like the mother with the small child. On the other hand, women who were self-affirming, were cast in the role of whore, witch and hag, feared and ridiculed. No wonder then that women developed a surrender mentality. In society they remained long without recourse to a court of law—didn't they ask to be raped and maimed and vilified and beaten? Didn't they willingly and knowingly comply?—and in churches they were counselled 'to bear their cross'.

Sexism results in the undervaluing of one half of humanity by defining the other half as superior; it wants and makes women the prisoners of their biology. Women were told their biology did not fit them for

1.   P. Neate, *The Guardian* (13 December 1988), quoting David Stayt of the Campaign for the Feminine Woman.

sporting activities, for intellectual pursuits such as mathematics, science and theology or, indeed, for independent living. Religions have reinforced this attitude by ascribing to women the narrowly prescribed roles of wife and mother that they abandon at their peril. Women, however, have felt a growing resentment at these narrow-minded views, which in reality impede women's actualization, the way women want to express themselves and want to live according to their God-given talents.

There is much harm done to women in the name of societal expectations and organized religion, with the former often greatly influenced by the latter. Christian prescriptions of 'appropriate' roles, which enable, for example, the Irish government to ban contraception and divorce or the Pope to advocate strongly a return to 'family values', or Jewish rules on periodical cleansing of women's 'impurity', or Islamic injunctions on the mobility of women, or Hindu demands of widow burning, and many more instances across cultures and religions, lower female self-esteem and show the variety of wrongs done to women. Further, there is the expectation by religious and societal leaders that women collude in the continuation of these prescriptions. However, women today, whether they are feminists or not and whether they follow their religion or not, no longer tolerate the very premises of their supposed inferiority.

In Christianity, secular moral guidelines based on the late antiquity understanding of biology and psychology came to define the role, the ability, the expectations of women, and even sexual codes of conduct. How extremely harmful this was to women is impressively demonstrated by Ute Ranke-Heinemann: Augustine's 'strict observance of contraceptive methods and attention to his partner's infertile days, foiled by the miscalculation that resulted in the birth of Adeodatus, was succeeded after his conversion by a fanatical campaign against contraception of all kinds' (1990: 65). The discussion on contraception produced some veritable mental contortions: 'The predominant view in antiquity was that of Aristotle, who held that the foetus did not develop a human soul for some time after conception, the male after forty days, the female after ninety. Prior to that it possessed a vegetable and then an animal soul (*Historia animalium* 7.3.583 b). This discrepancy between the origination of the male and the female soul was more than a span of time; it was also a measure of human quality because it indicated that the soul belonged to the man before the woman. The soul, meaning the essence of humanity, was something male rather than female' (Ranke-Heinemann 1990: 61). Woman is firmly held to be a second-class citizen, her power limited to sexuality. But then 'female power is regarded as dangerous and malevolent if it is not exercised in conjunction with the male and under his control' (Kumari 1988–89: 23).

Worst of all, women are dissatisfied with their own sex and believe men when they denigrate women. There are many examples of this. We want to quote an interesting one from Nigeria (Pro Mundi Vita, Dossier, Africa, 9 October 1979) which reports on a survey of Nigerians of all ages. The question: 'If you could be born again, would you choose to be a man or a woman?' was answered in the following way:

by	Boys	Girls	Men	Women
'as a man'	92.6%	47.5%	88.6%	57.1%
'as a woman'	6.1%	43.1%	1.0%	31.8%
'no reply'	1.7%	9.3%	10.2%	11.0%

We all know of women who believe that their sex does not make good doctors, lawyers, engineers, dentists, scientists, theologians or clergy. Where did they get these ideas from and why do they hold them? Further, how is it possible for women to believe other women deserve violence from their husbands or sexual harassment from strangers in the street or the men they work for? How is it that women can dislike their own bodies and only find them worthy if they fit a distorted picture produced by men? Frightening statistics are coming to light to show how models maintain their figures through abuse of drugs, yet this destructive and 'unnatural' figure is projected as ideal.

Throughout history, however, there have been women who have doubted the wisdom of societal and clerical prescriptions and who have found their full humanity outside the allocated narrow slot. They did not conform to a formula of beauty and acceptability. They were independent, articulate, wilful women who dared to dissent, to go their own way, to interpret their life free from the strictures of societies into which they were born. They found that they could be poetesses, prophetesses, queens and rulers, writers and painters, doctors and educators, single women and mothers, lay and religious, politicians and beggars. Many of these women contributed significantly in different areas of life (Rowbotham 1976). Yet it is these women who were and are accused of selfishness, materialism and a lack of the so-called 'feminine' virtues of altruism and true motherhood. They were exhorted to immolate their independence on the altars of respectability as defined by men. Yet, they had the courage and gift to step outside the protected male-defined sphere.

It is women then who in stepping outside the stereotypes are perceived as the problem. They are cast in the role of unruly women, dangerous and shrill. We have been so used to the silence of women in church and state that women only whispering are perceived as being shrill. Women who only want to be 'feminine' do not step out of their role play; they are proud of their station in life and very often they are the most vociferous voices against women who find their full humanity in the narrow slot allocated to woman by society, as well as going beyond it in order to be accepted as they are and not done up to conform to a formula of beauty and acceptability. It will take these women longest to understand the extent of their dependency and captivity.

So what Do we Say of Us?

The reclaiming of history by women is enabling us to explore and to explode many patriarchal myths about women's place and capabilities. We have laboured a long time under the 'Tarzan myth', condemning women to sit coyly at home tending the baby while 'he-man' went out in search of food. She was passive; he was active in protecting the human race. It is not our intention to examine extensively research on pre-history and the origins of division of labour along gender lines; we wish only to say that 'man the hunter' was not the whole story; it is simply a role patriarchy assumes for allocating a passive place to woman. A truer picture would be that the life-sustaining activity was first the gathering, then the planting carried out by the women, in addition to child-minding. The hunting was a bonus; it supplemented the stocks. Woman shared with man; both were instrumental in ensuring the survival of the clan; her role was an active, not a passive one.

If we doubt the abilities of women, their intellectual capacities, we need only look as a case in point to Aphra Ben, a prolific feminist writer of the seventeenth century. She wrote 13 novels some 30 years before Daniel Defoe wrote *Robinson Crusoe*, which has been heralded as the first novel in English, and 17 plays in as many years. She was also an adventuress, who in the West Indies became involved in a slave rebellion, a spy for Charles II and a political activist. She was successful in her day as a writer and thinker, yet the establishment, the dominant force in history, has buried her achievements (Spender 1982a: 30). It has attempted to do the same with an endless list of women, including Mary Wollstonecroft, Mary Astell, Catherine Macauley and Olympe de Gouges (Spender 1982a: 547-48).

Where women's capabilities are circumscribed by biological givens it is usually to enforce some restriction upon women. Women are the weaker sex and so must be 'protected'—here one could read 'restricted'. Again a casual glance at history illustrates the folly of this argument. The first laurel wreath in the original Olympics went to a Macedonian woman who beat all the male charioteers. Although this may not be altogether liberating for contemporary women, if we look to Sojourner Truth we see clearly how we have been given false information and believed it. Addressing a women's convention in 1851, she said: 'Nobody ever helped me into carriages or over mud puddles, or gave me the best place. And ain't I a woman?...I can work as much and eat as much as any man when I can get it and bear the lash as well. And ain't I a woman? I have borne 13 children and seen most of them sold off to slavery, and when I cried out with a mother's grief, none but I heard me. And ain't I a woman?' (Harrison 1985: 9).

The myth of the 'helpless female' is exactly that and has never applied to women in disadvantaged groups, be they black or working class. These women have always worked as physically hard as men and dealt with motherhood as well; pregnant women pulled coal trucks along underground tracks in Welsh mines and, as we have seen from the quote, no allowances were made for women in slavery because of their sex. To see women as weak, incapable beings, is a myth that serves two purposes for patriarchy: first, it keeps women out of certain 'male preserves', thus reducing competition; secondly, it allows women who are wives to become symbols of male power. If men can keep their wives 'at home' in comfort, it shows they must have money, and some status. A working wife, on the other hand, unless it is voluntary work, casts economic aspersions on her husband.

Women have been rulers, sometimes fierce (Boadicea), sometimes wise (Elizabeth I), sometimes foolish (Cleopatra). Women have been painters, warriors, poets, chemists. Indeed, women have been successful in all walks of life. It would help women's self-affirmation if other women were placed before them as examples. We know we are strong, intelligent, wise, diplomatic and creative. We find ourselves agreeing with Sojourner Truth: 'If the first woman God ever made was strong enough to turn the world upside down all alone, these women all together ought to be able to turn it back and get it right side up again! And now they is asking to do it, men better let 'em' (Spender 1982a: 267).

The Women's Movement

The contemporary women's movement has forerunners in history both in the religious and secular field, despite a patriarchal faith system. Women's religious authority in Christianity, teaching the faith to their children and exceptionally so to adults, caring for the young and the old and the weak in their communities in the name of Jesus, praying and following practical and intellectual pursuits, has never been totally eradicated. Secular feminism is nothing new either. It goes back to thinkers such as Mary Wollstonecraft and her 'Vindications of the Rights of Women' in 1792, which is an analysis of the situation of women and their demands for better education, legal and economic reforms, as well as to women campaigning for the abolition of slavery, the Grimké sisters Sarah and Angelina in the nineteenth century in the US; to Elisabeth Cady Stanton with the publication of her *Woman's Bible* in 1898 and to Simone de Beauvoir with *The Second Sex*, published in 1949. In many instances one cannot make a hard and fast separation between religious and secular feminism, as the goals of feminism, inclusiveness and inter-connectedness, are 'ecumenical', all-embracing goals.

Throughout history women have had to fight to participate, to enter debate in public, to be heard, to be seen. When they have tried, they have been ridiculed and told it was virtuous not to be selfish and told to look after others. The churches have sanctioned this view by calling it God-given, and natural for woman to regard herself as of little value and to continue in the service of others.

One shift that has happened in the secular world has been the idea that every individual and not the family is responsible for himself or herself. The individual, rather than the family, is now the smallest unit of society. The myth of the family as the building block of society has long been used to keep women in 'their' place, that is at home, to produce the next generation and to spend themselves in the nurturing roles necessary for this task. Role models in society inculturate women to internalize the understanding of what women 'ought' to be rather than what women are. Sex role stereotypes, sweetly smiling females, neatly turned out and proportioned, ever submissive, docile, helpful, as if developed according to a formula, replicate the pattern of domination and subordination: if one sex is defined as being submissive, if stress is laid on this quality, then it follows that the other sex is rightfully dominant.

An important development away from the dominance-submission model was the franchise debate that catapulted women's aspirations and men's restrictions on these aspirations into the open. But it was not only men who opposed women's franchise; women themselves at the beginning of the twentieth century were not convinced that it was in their interest to become independent. The Committee for Opposing Female Suffrage, mindful 'That the time has now arrived when it is incumbent on those who believe that the extension of the franchise to women would be contrary to the best interests of the country and the empire' invited women to unite in their fight against it.[2] The Women's Anti-Suffrage League pointed out, that it was 'of fundamental importance for the national welfare that the spirit of sex antagonism which is being aroused by much of the women's suffrage propaganda, should be combated by recognition of the fact, that the respective spheres of men and women are neither antagonistic nor identical but complementary'.[3]

This is a good example of the 'biology is destiny' argument. The female sex has to complement the male sex; the woman is here to serve the man not as equal but in a relationship of dependence. The 'complementarity' argument is faulty because it means neither men nor women are 'whole' individual entities, indivisible and autonomous. It is faulty because society is composed of individuals who are whole, and not families, which are divisible.

World War II had a dramatic impact on the lives of most women because their labours were needed outside the home as part of the war effort. When the war was over and women's work was surplus to demand, they did not go back to being full-time housewives. Their demands for work outside the home triggered social change. The outcome has been equality with men before the law and equal pay. But despite the changes in the law, many women find that now they have a dual role as both breadwinner and housekeeper. Sadly the latter has not changed over the years.

Talk of 'emancipation' meant women stepping into jobs and professions traditionally held by men. Women in the workforce were necessarily seen as competing with men. This development gave women a certain degree of autonomy and at the same time brought them into conflict with male dominated systems. Many professions, for example

2.   Founding Resolution 3.12.1908 (Fawcett Library, London).
3.   Letter inviting women to become members, autumn 1907 (Fawcett Library, London).

teaching, still demanded that women gave up their work once they married and despite being given access to academic institutions women were often denied the qualification—in Cambridge until 1947 (Storkey 1985: 24). Women began to realize that however competent they were, promotion could still be denied them, and usually, if they had to look after young children, their home circumstances were cited as a reason for non-advancement in their career. While employers will be less open about children and family as reasons for non-advancement it still remains true that women are disadvantaged at work. The latest figures regarding university employment show that a very small percentage of women rise to the higher grades, despite having a very high profile in their fields. The matter of pay gives no better a story, with women earning less for the same jobs. A woman in clerical work is likely to earn £125,000 less in the course of her working life then her male colleagues. The figure is higher for those in shop work who are likely to lose out to the tune of £250,000 over a working life.[4] The same report cited the case of a female solicitor who was replaced during maternity leave by a man with less experience who carried the same work load—he was paid £10,000 a year more for the same job! Clearly the matter of pay and position is not yet solved. When we look at the Episcopalian/Anglican churches we see very much the same story: there are a high number of non-stipendary women priests and very few women in senior positions. There are, however, as many female church cleaners and flower arrangers as ever!

When the women's movement initially began to investigate the grievances of women in these areas, it began to realize that the problems went very deep. The way society behaves and is run came under scrutiny. The systems seemed to deny the autonomy of the individual to be self-directed. The experience that women underwent of being 'objects' in various systems led the women's movement to declare that such 'object-making' is wrong and so for some women the emphasis shifted from equal access to the systems to changing the systems. Women felt they had legitimate claims that were overlooked and they believed that their opinions about these matters were worthy of consideration.

If the argument, not the authority, is to count then those in authority begin to feel threatened. If the lawmakers in society decree and prescribe role models and attitudes of behaviour, but if these prescriptions are not

4. *The Daily Express*, 'Women Earn £250,000 Less Than Men' (20 February 2000): 8, reporting latest government statistics.

followed any longer, if their 'authority' is not accepted or if their arguments are shown to be false in the light of experience, who or what then constitutes authority? From this starting point, the investigation of authority, the women's movement began to investigate the relationship between men and women and found it faulty. In the context of the patriarchal notions of 'do's' and 'dont's', of the projection of spheres of action 'proper' to each sex, of the roles women and men 'ought' to play in society, to uphold a male-run system, the women's movement set out to break down the demarcation lines in society by pointing out the injustice inherent in them. 'Abusive authority' in secular and religious spheres provokes revolution. 'Certainly, it does not do so consciously. Yet its style of life and way of ruling finally become a provocation. This occurs when a feeling of impunity takes root among the elite: We are allowed anything, we can do anything. This is a delusion' (Kapuscinski 1986: 11). It is then the bridle of authority that becomes intolerable, the application of 'power over' that is resisted. Once we realize this, to step out of the shadow of authority is important, to break one's routine is important. It is not the solution, but the first stepping stone towards it.

If we look at examples of abusive relationships from cultures around the world, we see how deep-seated the inequality between the sexes is. If creativity is castrated, as is the case with genital mutilation and female circumcision in Northern African societies, if women strangle their daughters at birth because society views female birth as a shame as in pre-Christian Europe and in some societies in China and India, intimidation and violence done in the name of tradition, even more so religious tradition, act as controls of behaviour. These examples from religions and cultures around the world should not obscure the fact that Christianity, the religious tradition of Europe, is not blameless in its dealing with women.

Christianity has always encouraged women to sacrifice themselves for love. The model of a good Christian women is the one who asks little and sacrifices much for Jesus and her family. Women who take a little for themselves often feel guilty and can suffer low self esteem as a result. This love trap is pernicious. Some feminist theologians are attempting to counter the notion of self-sacrificial love with that of eros, the dynamic self-affirming love of which Heyward speaks (1989) but the churches have not yet caught on to this. Of course, a more concrete example of Christianity's abuse of women is the witch craze of the sixteenth and seventeenth centuries, in which 90 per cent of the victims were women.

While this frenzy for blood letting has abated, the sexual stereotyping that was at the root of many of the persecutions has not. Independent women are still viewed with suspicion, indeed, the modern film industry shouts that message loud and clear.

Still in our times, in societies that have strong 'traditional' views on purity and pollution, women's access to economic and political resources is controlled and restricted. In the Latin American tradition this is called 'machismo', the cluster of male traits related to masculine honour which requires emphasis of gender differences and constant reinforcing of traditional roles. It will effect birth control decisions within and outside marriage. Paternity, illegitimate and legitimate, becomes a source of pride, a symbol of potency, 'a target of respect but seldom of responsibility'. Maleness is glorified, femaleness denigrated. The recent development in mobile Doppler scanning, the test done to check a baby in utero, has found questionable use in Indian villages where fees are charged to establish the sex of the baby, and as a consequence female foetuses are then often aborted. Female life is also cheap in the Western world where spousal murder rates are frighteningly high. In Britain two women a week are murdered by partners or ex-partners, while in America the figure is 12 women per week (Home Office 1999). This is scandalous enough, but the fact that these figures are buried in a report and not more easily accessible to people is even more worrying. Female bodies are also considered to be public property. We are now being told that the annual rape figures for Britain are more like 300,000 than the 25,000 reported. The increase is said to be in so-called date rape, the hardest to prosecute. At the same time that these figures were released two senior academics in the US proposed that rape is an evolutionary activity and therefore natural.[5] This moves the debate back from viewing rape as an act of violence and into the 'man can't help himself' bracket that feminists and others have fought so hard to disprove. The churches still remain silent on these matters.

One of the aims of feminist theologies is to base the social identity of women and men on the concept of the personhood of the individual. This would mean an end to the role-playing that assumes that each sex is only capable of certain actions and inhabits separate spheres. 'To expand the space we share' is a good description of the aims of feminism, ultimately the recognition that no space should be exclusive to one sex and that the bodies of women are not, as a matter of fact, at the service of

5.   *The Times Higher Educational Supplement* (4 February 2000): 49.

men, be it domestically or sexually. This will be a difficult lesson to learn and a very hard reality to unpick as so much of our society depends on unequal labour and free access to women.

Women and Religion

Although the theological and social examination of the place of women in religion goes back to the nineteenth century, and in some cases beyond, the real challenge arose in the twentieth century. It would be hard to argue that the rise of feminist consciousness in the 1950s was fuelled by its nineteenth-century foremother since much of the work of Elizabeth Cady Stanton and others was long forgotten. Most of the momentum came from the Civil Rights Movement. Christian women who had been demonstrating and campaigning for the rights of black citizens found, when they returned to their churches, that their rights were not always respected. Further, that any claims they made for equality were taken less seriously then those of their black colleagues. In addition Christian women were being told of the value of their own experience by their secular sisters and having that experience totally ignored by their own faith communities. This situation encouraged many women interested in theology and religion to think in a highly critical way for the first time about the traditions in which they found themselves.

There is no doubt that these women felt the same frustrations as their nineteenth-century sisters did but there were more routes open to them than to their foresisters. Not only could they gain theological education, although this was not as easy as we may think, but there were new theological tools available in the form of liberation and process theology (these will be discussed in Chapter 4). Nevertheless, the model of sexual politics with its division of labour along gender lines was the prevailing model in societies and churches.

Today sex discrimination is still with us in some churches, despite legislation forbidding sex discrimination in secular professions. The Catholic and Orthodox churches still refuse to ordain women despite rhetoric about the equality of all and a formal and public apology for the way it has treated women through its history. It still does not fundamentally aim at inclusion of women but at exclusion. The result is inequality, which, in the field of the churches, is not so much the result of a division of labour (although that is part of it) as that of maintaining the balance of power. Power ensures privilege as much in society as in churches and many in the churches do not want to abandon that.

A glaring example is the address called 'Domestic Collaborators in the Priesthood' by Pope John Paul II. He assured 4000 women, who came on a pilgrimage to Rome as an international group of priests' housekeepers, that they were involved in a 'great cause' well-suited to their 'female charisms': 'Let me confide that upon seeing you here in such great numbers and from several countries of Europe and even Madagascar, my first impression is: Women do have their place in the church!' He urged the women: 'Be happy that you can keep the residence of the priest clean, and free him from the material tasks which would absorb part of the time that he so needs for his apostolic labours' and 'You can never thank the Lord enough for giving you the grace of choosing to serve the clergy'.[6] As so many witty cartoons have shown, women's place in this church is on their knees, cleaning, flower arranging, waiting on clergy. The Pope sadly does not elaborate why women's charisms should embrace cleaning and men's charisms apostolic labours—he does not need to; he is clear in his mind that this is a legitimate division of labour.

In the context of theology women have encountered institutional sexism, the power of traditional theology, which we call patriarchal theology. Pronouncements that force women to live an intolerably restricted life, regulated and declared 'God-given', are damaging to women. But such is the extent of patriarchal power that women have internalized these demands of restriction and so many of them have never developed a positive self-image.

In Christianity, theology has been a male preserve; women were excluded from the study of it until a generation ago. As recently as the beginning of this century women were described in the *Catholic Encyclopaedia* as 'inferior to the male sex, both as regards body and soul'.[7] The theory, espoused by the *Catholic Encyclopaedia*, of the organic conception of society, of the complementarity of the sexes and of the reciprocity of services rendered meant that women did not need to engage in advanced studies and were therefore excluded from ordained ministry.

How far are the churches in the twenty-first century, directed by traditional theologians, capable of re-interpreting the gospel in a way that makes it possible to overcome this kind of narrow, faulty, dualistic thinking? Today it is no longer a question whether one is for or against

---

6. Extract from the USA Bulletin of St Joan's International Alliance, June 1982 (Fawcett Library, London).

7. *Catholic Encyclopaedia* XV (1912): 687-98 (688).

feminism and indeed Christian feminism, but a question of how soon the church hierarchies accept Christian feminism in the light of the gospel message. Feminist theology points to new forms of communities of equals through which the faith can be transmitted away from perpetuating structural injustices and towards a greater human development in justice and peace. But are the churches, when confronted with the political situation in society and with all the problems of social change, sufficiently galvanized to respond to the hopes, frustrations and anxieties of the people, when the challenge is to stand in unconditional solidarity with the real interests of the people?

These are very important issues given the radical vision of the equal worth of everybody and the realization of making use of one's God-given talents. We must beware of a development where all feminist manifestations will as of right be dictated exclusively by women theorists who think that their views are of more value than those of the rank and file and thereby are just repeating the pattern of the patriarchal societies. Therefore, academic study is needed in feminism and particularly in feminist theology to reflect critically upon the direction of research, ensuring that the patterns we are criticizing are not repeated. But beyond this specialization a penetrating rethink in society at large, with law-makers, leaders, writers, teachers and social workers is required to change public perception of women's worth. The women's movement is a movement of women, not just of experts; by giving space and time to everybody involved in furthering its aims, it will become the space in which new forms are tried and tested in the search for new norms.

Women want to move from exclusion to inclusion. They want to make it possible for society to stop exclusion techniques and distancing mechanisms that are to the detriment of society. In the churches women demand an end to ritual invisibility and sexism through withholding access to all positions from them.

Christian churches are notoriously selective about tradition; moreover, Jesus said 'I am the Truth'; he did not say 'I am the Tradition'. The arguments of so-called 'traditionalists' often reveal themselves as arguments of people who are very ignorant of 'tradition'. What is more, they declare cultural conditions of a relatively short span of time as 'tradition', making out that 'traditional values' are eternal and God-given. What they call 'tradition' is merely a culturally conditioned convention. In fact, very often something termed 'the tradition' was nothing like it; for example compulsory priestly celibacy in the RC

Church, which, as a practice, became normative only about 1100 years after Jesus. Tradition is very often a culturally determined convention that has very little to do with the values and visions of Christ. Tradition cannot necessarily be said to be orthodox either, as it stems from a certain situation in society that might have nothing to do with the gospel truth of 'Love one another!'. The prohibition on the ordination of women to the priesthood for example, cannot be squared with Christ's teaching and cannot be supported by a single biblical quote.

Christian feminists can call a 'Christian tradition' that which values everybody equally and works for non-violent solutions by overcoming secular divisions in the love of Christ. But stereotyping of women in the name of tradition, withholding of education from women, or justifying the endurance of physical pain or the continuation in public of a marriage that has broken down, to name but a few, shows a one-sided and wrong application of tradition which can by no means be called 'Christian'.

The stress in traditional theology on taking power or initiative away from the individual in the name of tradition, produced an ethic of being victim, of accepting being an object, but not a subject, an agent of one's own talents. Instead of respect, growth, potential, the stress has been on guilt, fear, hell and damnation. Therefore feminism could also be called an ethic of risk taking, the risks involved from being on the margin of the decision-making processes and not centre-stage. It is risk taking because it challenges 'tradition'; it is risk taking because it actually unmasks the harm that is done in the name of tradition.

On an everyday level, women want to go out and earn a living, to become independent and self-supporting, and they often face sexual harassment and verbal abuse that is demeaning to any self-respecting woman. Yet many women daily take that risk. That it is the men who pose the danger 'outside' (rape, assault, sexual harassment, verbal abuse), does not seem to come into the calculation. Rape and especially the fear of rape, powerfully reinforces the injunction on leaving the house. Rape, thus, is perceived not to be a horrible crime and experience, but a punishment on those who have ventured out, who have been dis-obedient and do not deserve any better. The women who are willing to step outside are taking a risk.

This realization has shaped a threefold approach to promoting the aims of feminism: resistance to societal prescriptions that are harmful to the body and mind of women, solidarity with those sharing the same predicament, in this country and abroad, and the creation of a community of equals. Or to put it differently: rejection of traditional interpretations that have shown themselves to be defining women by their biological roles alone and projection of alternatives and action in the pursuit of this goal. One has to denounce before one can announce, but denounce, announce and proclaim we must.

In order to achieve their goal, women paradoxically have to demand precisely what they want to overcome: power, but understood not as power over others, but as power for achieving change. Therefore it is really an empowerment that unlocks the potential inherent in everybody and that can change the structures accordingly. Janet Morley puts it like this in one of her prayers: 'We have used our power to dominate and our weakness to manipulate' (1988: 33). Women have believed what patriarchy in society and religion has told them: the women-at-home-model is the moral redeemer model that attributes to the subordinated female a very powerful role, a moral force which is lacking in the dominant male. The you-must-not-swear-in-front-of-the-ladies syndrome, every woman called a lady, men acting out certain acts of chivalry, oozing old-worldly charm, because women are the charming, helpless creatures, possessed by moral fortitude, the shining examples to many a faltering man, are the psychological props for the women at home. Compliant women act out the role play of moral redeemer versus the male role play of a man is a man is a man or boys will be boys model. The role play of the male being a rascal and the woman being the good wife at home is the stuff of which Hollywood films are made, but this role play does not tally with reality. It is fantasy: woman is conceded a moral force but only when she is in place, in her home, under control. A woman's morality is seen in reverse once she leaves that sphere—a woman outside the home is prey as she is viewed as courting violence and violation.

William Kennedy Smith, charged with the crime of rape, was acquitted in the US in December 1991 and the newspapers censured feminists who were stung by the verdict. It was a woman who toed the male party line by writing 'The act of unwanted sex with a known man is not in itself intrinsically traumatic, although it may be unpleasant.' (Amiel 1991). A woman who speaks of rape as 'not intrinsically traumatic' displays how much the male fantasies of purity at home and pollution outside it have been internalized by large sectors of society. A woman on her own must be morally dubious. The task for the future must be to present an alternative model. Women do not want power to dominate and to hide behind their weakness in order to manipulate their environment or religions; they do not want prescriptions about what they can and cannot do and what hurts and what does not hurt; their vision is a vision of transformation, in which these operations are eliminated.

Any community draws its strength from the diversity of its members, their bonding and acceptance and needs. A theology that tells people that it is 'good' to suffer, to be a victim, to make sacrifices, usually somebody else's sacrifices, overlooks the unique diverse gifts and talents that remain unlocked. Feminist theology is engaged therefore in exploring how to unlock women's and men's potential away from conforming to a system, how to find personal fulfilment, going beyond surviving a system to living a faith. Accepting a system that is based on self-oppression reveals nothing but insecurity and fear of one's own freedom. This is the cul-de-sac of authoritarian centralism in societies and churches. Authoritarianism is flourishing when the power of decision making of all groups is taken over by one group exclusively and every 'rejuvenation', 'modernization', 'aggiornamento', is instituted from above. In the RC Church the fixation on authority, centralized authority vested in the Pope, leads from time to time to attempts at rejuvenation from above; various councils and synods meet from time to time, with the result that the system as such wins, not the individual, because measures are taken for and not by the individual believer.

The system not only wins, but demands obedience. But faith cannot be demanded. Facile promises of other-worldly reward and redemption ring hollow to women who are called upon to make 'sacrifices', to be obedient, to forego leading a fulfilling life. The obedient cannot change things sufficiently because they collaborate in the system, and collaboration leads to compromises. Would Jesus have changed anything had he just 'collaborated'? (Drewermann 1990: 133).

Patriarchal Theology—Guilty but Redeemable?

Feminists distinguish between patriarchal and feminist theology in order to denote what limits women's full participation in patriarchal theology and what contributes to women's full participation as envisaged by feminist theology. Patriarchal theology stands in need of critical reassessment so as to make visible the richness of scriptures, the all-inclusiveness of teaching and the all-embracing vision of participation by everybody.

What we mean is that the teaching of 'love your neighbour', the absolute acceptance without reservation of everybody as equal, the acceptance of everybody as neighbour, has been eroded by an interpretation that has made distinctions between 'friend' and 'foe', insider and outsider, 'Christian' and 'Non-Christian', male and female. We must not gloss over in the long history of Christianity the very un-Christian activities of popes preaching the Crusades, when Christian slaughtered Muslims and Jews, of the Inquisition, when Christians investigated, tortured and handed over for execution fellow Christians not found to be Christian enough, of the witch hunts, when Christians investigated, tortured and handed over for execution fellow Christians judged to be in union with the Devil, of the factional purges in the name of rooting out 'heresies' by many a medieval bishop and pope, of papal anti-semitism and papal silence when confronted with anti-semitism. In the history of Christianity, forceful baptisms of whole peoples such as the pagan Saxons in the eighth century or the rebaptism of Orthodox Christian Serbs as Roman Catholics in World War II or the stark alternatives of accepting baptism or expulsion presented to the Jews in Spain in 1492, show that the teaching of the Sermon on the Mount was blatantly disregarded by the very church which based its values on the Sermon on the Mount.

Many people argue that all these 'deviations' were products of their time, that they have to be seen in their historical context. We agree wholeheartedly with these qualifications. But today, because women have realized how badly they have been treated, they can make the connection and see how badly others have been treated because racist and sexist interpretations prevailed. Once you allow yourself to think in two categories, 'them' and 'us', the polarization into friend and foe starts. It produces a vicious circle with no way out. By cataloguing such gross deviations we want to show that the patriarchal interpretation of theology, what is licit in the name of 'God', has been abusive.

Christianity has been guilty of a number of historically conditioned discriminations; it has interferred in the politics of nations and it has been guilty of racism, the prejudice that one race is better than another one and it is still guilty of sexism. Identifying and denouncing such gross behaviour is the first necessary step on the way to dealing with it. The space is cleared to start discovering and proclaiming what is positive in the social teaching of Christianity.

Prophetic voices on equality, on ending prejudice, on understanding that all creation is connected, have come from various quarters, rising out of their particular situation, pointing to the inequality in society and relationships, the abuse of power in political systems and the ambivalence of the attitude of institutional churches and religious systems. After the experience of two world wars in the twentieth century, traditional theologies of triumphalism and fundamentalism and certainties of superiority have come under scrutiny. Out of an abusive political situation liberation theology was born in Latin American societies. Black Theology analyzed racial discrimination in unequal power systems and Creation Spirituality inspired reflection and engendered a rethink about the harmful consequences of our quest to 'dominate' the earth and its resources.

With the emergence of feminist theory, women and men have applied feminist thought to the task of doing theology, which enables them to look at women's realities from a theological point of view, so far overlooked by liberation and black theologies. Feminist theology takes as its starting point the experience of women and men and their interaction with each other and with society, as source from which to do theology. We see the stress shift from authority, imposed from outside, to self authority, striven for throughout life. This in turn can effect the political realm and the way life is viewed. The most often quoted example of Christianity learning from a social situation is the example of slavery. The Christian churches in the wake of secular legislation did shed the millennia-old view that slavery was instituted by God and accepted that slavery was an evil institution created by fellow human beings and that it needed to be abolished. Christianity has shown itself capable of change, of shedding dearly-held views when progress in science and societies at large has shown a particular theological tenet to be wrong.

An exciting theological landscape is opening up before us with women around the world taking the initiative, applying their experience to so-called truths of theology. Much of this work springs from a post-colonial critique as well as from standard liberation theology. This is very clear in Asia where theologians have pointed out that the struggles of the people have been hindered by the colonial Christ, a Christ who carries the agenda of another culture and a conquering one at that. Under the weight of critical analysis based in peoples experience, the Christ is being transformed from that of the universal absolutes of conquering armies to the unfolding healer in the midst of a broken community, from the Lord of all to the dispossessed peasant woman clinging to the grains of survival, from the unchanging Saviour to the cries of the not yet saved and from the blood of eternal salvation to the salvific blood of history' (Isherwood 1999: 127).

Of course, this assumes a tremendous power shift and one that we can only welcome. It destabilises hierarchies and all that depends on them and gives voice to the people. It also challenges the cultural constructions that have been possible through the lens of Christianity and Greek dualism which is so endemic within it. Asian women suffered the pain of re-definition under the colonizing Christ: they were not only inferior because they were the 'pagan' other but also because they were women. Mary John Mananzan demonstrates how this led to a reduction in their status in Filipino society. Before the conquest women were understood as the sole generators of life and as such were given very high status. They were not under the authority of men and sexual mores were far less restrictive. They also held power in the area of religion. With the coming of the Spanish and Christianity all that disappeared. However, by reconnecting with their pre-colonial past many Christian Filipino women are challenging the received tradition and bring the whole debate into the open. They regain their humanness, which is no small matter under a system that has denied it for so long, and standing as embodied challenges to all that would reduce them (Isherwood 1999: 120-21).

Similar patterns are emerging with women in Latin America, Europe, the US, and South Africa, all questioning 'givens' and celebrating new realities. Many of these movements do not consider themselves to be feminist or theological, for example, women's land movements such as those of Chiapas or the Chipko women of India who understand their agendas in a very practical and life sustaining way. They do not have the luxury of time to define their philosophical/theological motivation. These movements very clearly demonstrate how taking one's own life experience as the basis for action can and does bring about enormous change in the face of overwhelming odds.

In many places throughout the world patriarchal theology is creaking under the weight of the lived experience of women and men. This is not to suggest that patriarchy is dead or even that it is dying, rather that alternatives are being sought by those on the margins to make sense out of the harsh realities of many lives. Indeed, patriarchy is being named as the cause of much of the hardship. Christian women in India are, for example, reclaiming the female power of Shakti, the divine energy, in order to maintain a sense of well being amidst the more rampant excesses of patriarchy. Perhaps surprisingly in an Indian context feminist theologians are able to make connections between the salvific blood of Jesus and the menstrual blood of women (Isherwood 1999: 127). Thus the very blood that has excluded women for so long from rituals and rites as it is seen as impure now provides a connection with Christianity. Women's blood places before us the many injustices that the female body has to suffer in a rigidly misogynistic society, the unwanted abortions because the child carried is the 'wrong sex', the beatings, the poverty and the exploitation in sex and labour. Through this challenge the blood of women becomes a sacramental sign of living community and not a stain of exclusion.

Latin American women engage Jesus in their struggle to a much greater degree than patriarchy has ever dared, that is to say they do not envisage a naive happy ending brought about by the intervention of God, but rather they engage with Jesus as a companion who is 'embedded' in their daily fight for life. This challenges the illusions that patriarchy uses to keep the status quo in place and to keep those in dire circumstances from rebellion through promises of eschatological Disney World. This more honest engagement with the harsh realities of life serves to resurrect something of the political impetus of the early Jesus movement, it saves us from the reversals of reality upon which patriarchy rests.

Feminist engagement with theology does not mean that patriarchy is vanquished but it does provide alternate ways of knowing, springing, as they do, from very diverse life experiences. This engagement does not mean that patriarchal theology is in some way absolved for the sins of the past and present played out on the bodies of women and men because of its myopic vision. What it does mean is that the future may, in part, be less abusive and more open to a divine conversation that includes all, rather than the divine monologue that excludes many. As feminist theology continues to uphold the cause of women, patriarchal religions will surely have to admit that once again they have been in error, this time in advocating sexism and silencing the voices of women. We therefore need to look at how sexism became entrenched in patriarchal religion.

Chapter 2

Patriarchal Theology and the Conditioning of Society

The Eve Trap

Societal and ecclesiastical norms do not simply materialize from thin air, they are fashioned by deeply held convictions and prior circumstances. The norms of the Western world have been greatly influenced by its Judaeo-Christian heritage.

If we open windows on the past and look carefully at what it has to tell the present, we enter into a living relationship with the past. It is a way of experiencing the past by allowing it to inhabit the present. Thus the past becomes accessible and contiguous and we understand better the development of ideas and concepts that are still shaping our thoughts today. The main source for the past among Christians is the Bible, but it is not just a holy book; it is a book with a political mission. Many feminist biblical scholars have engaged in critical investigation of what the Bible tells us and what it does not tell us, what has been added, differently interpreted and translated in the long history of its use, and what has been redacted out.

Just a cursory look at the creation story in Genesis shows us that the Judaeo-Christian sources seek to explain the creation in a manner distinctly different from creation myths from other Western Asiatic and Northern African societies of the time. These other creation myths are accounts of how the world came to be and they speak of a mystical fusion of male and female deities, of the joint workings of male and female deities (cf. Reeves-Sanday 1981: 219). They would not be easily explicable, comprehensive or acceptable otherwise. These accounts also try to explain the riddle of the origin of the One and its diversification into many. The biblical agenda does not go as far, yet at the same time goes further. In the Genesis story the female agency is redacted out, God is firmly a 'He' who engenders offspring without apparently active female participation. 'God brooding over the waters' is the expression used, which denoted for readers versed in Near Eastern literary sources the perfect way of fusion of the male and female—namely water—principle. The accounts go on to explain how good and evil came into the world which was created a 'paradise'—a Persian word for walled garden—by a male God. Mary Daly notes in this context that 'paradise', an enclave, something walled in and self contained, could not have been enough for Eve who would have wished to explore it further, since seeking knowledge through understanding one's environment is a human activity (Daly 1973: 66). The Judaeo-Christian creation mythology speaks not only of the complex riddle of creation itself, but of the exclusively one creator, who is male, and sets out what is 'good' and what is 'evil'. God as male is the mirror image of a patriarchal society in which the leaders of the tribes are men, who rule and judge. The context in which the creation account was written reflects the—male—Priestly Writers and the political agenda of Jewish—male—monotheism meant the domination of woman by man.

Despite the fact that Genesis carries two creation stories, neither overtly requires the participation of the female in order to create. Rosalind Miles speaks of the limitations of monotheism as she perceives it, not only as a theology, but as a power relation: 'Any one God idea has a built-in notion of primacy and supremacy... As a power relation then, monotheism inevitably creates a hierarchy' (1989: 92) and we might add, a male hierarchy, of course. In considering the God of Israel, we are introduced to a male God who has given woman a 'life sentence of second order existence', because, in the words of Miles, 'If God was male and woman was not male, then whatever God was, woman was not' (1989: 93). The power relation of monotheism is asymmetrical.

The first account, in Gen. 1.26-27, says:

> Then God said, 'Let us make man in our image, after our likeness; and let them have dominion over the fish of the sea, and over the bird of the air, and over the cattle, and over all the earth, and over every creeping thing that creeps upon the earth'. So God created man in his own image, in the image of God he created him; male and female he created them.

The second account deals with the creation of man separately from the creation of the woman. We read in Gen. 2.21-23:

> So the Lord God caused a deep sleep to fall upon the man, and while he slept took one of his ribs, and closed up its place with flesh; and the rib which the Lord God had taken from the man, he made into a woman

and brought her to the man. Then the man said, 'This at last is bone of my bones and flesh of my flesh; she shall be called Woman, because she was taken out of man.'

The first account imputes no inferiority to the woman, but the second one does. It is no surprise that under male monotheism the story suggesting equal creation under God was quickly forgotten. It would have served no useful purpose for patriarchy to remember it.

Miles finds the creation story a negation of evolution and biology: 'God reverses biology and stands nature on its head with the birth of a manchild, in defiance of evolution, where men and women evolved together and of life itself, where woman gives birth to man' (1989: 95). She refers to the Adam and Eve story as 'possibly the most effective piece of enemy propaganda in the long history of the sex war' (1989: 94), yet precisely this negation has become the accepted interpretation.

The message of women's inferiority is threefold in the creation story:

(1) God is solely male—Mary Daly's statement 'If God is male, then the male is God' is logical and persuasive (Daly 1973: 64).

(2) Woman is created from man and therefore is secondary in human creation, although, by an ascending order of creation, the last to be created, in fact, the final glory.

(3) The male God, having made the perfect world, has it shattered by disobedient woman.

This interpretation paints womanhood as something negative, at fault, needing supervision. From it springs a world of commentary, from the Jewish rabbis to the scholastics in the Middle Ages, in which it is taken for granted that women are essentially inferior to men. Woman is the temptress, the seductress, the polluter, and therefore in need of supervision by male masters. Division of labour would run along gender lines, and direct access to the deity would be denied to women. Uncleanliness taboos served as analogies for social order as the body was seen as a symbol of society (Reeves-Sanday 1981: 91). The body was viewed as unruly and therefore in need of regulation and control. Women's bodies with their involuntary changes were feared most and therefore seemed in most need of control.

The story of the Fall of man reinforces the bias. Miles argues that this event is rightly called the Fall of man, as Eve did not so much fall, but was pushed. Her reasons for declaring this are based on the background struggle at the time between goddess religion and the new male monotheism, which was trying to establish itself. This argument is developed further in the section on language; it is sufficient here to note that woman and the snake, both central to the story of the Fall, were primary symbols and agents of the goddess. As such Eve (woman) and the snake had to be vilified. Woman led innocent man to sin, she tempted him to go against the instructions of the male God and seek knowledge. The snake encourages Eve in her actions and she in turn brought about 'the Fall of Man'. Paradise is lost and God will eventually have to send His son as a blood sacrifice to atone for the evil in the world: the evil brought into the world by Eve (woman). It was this view of events that enabled Ambrose, many centuries later, to state: 'Adam was led to sin by Eve, not Eve by Adam. It is just and right then, that women accept as Lord and Master him who she led to sin' (Ranelagh 1985: 49).

This is strange logic since surely one would be ill-advised to accept as Master a character so easily led to sin. But more so, it overlooks the biblical evidence in Gen. 3.16, which shows how the fact that men rule over women is a result of a later development, the Fall. Traditionally this passage 'I will greatly multiply your pain in childbearing; in pain you shall bring forth children, yet your desire shall be for your husband, and he shall rule over you', has been quoted as the reason why man must 'lord it over' woman. Because of her unruly nature, woman was punished and henceforth needed to be controlled by man. But this does not follow in our understanding. The passage can equally be understood as the Fall causing the sin of sexism, the subjugation of woman, the 'individual degradation of one half of humanity on socio-biological grounds' (Illich 1983: 34).

Although the snake and Eve were in pursuit of the fruit of the tree of knowledge, the traditional interpretation of the story has usually claimed that sex was the cause of our downfall. Therefore, women have found themselves labelled as more material, physical and 'lusty' and this element within us has needed to be controlled since it brings punishment and chaos according to the Genesis story. Why this strand should be picked out of the story is difficult to comprehend unless the story is seen as not just myth but also polemic. The object of this polemic is a much older culture, that of the great mother. Christians are quick to forget the Babylonian background of these early writings and as such can easily overlook that there was another character in the original stories and that was the female divine. With the rise of patriarchal cultures it became important to have stories as well as practices that overthrew any previous understandings. There is much work that shows how this was done with the Genesis mythology (Long 1992; Westermann 1974). In short all that was valued by the goddess culture was vilified in the Priestly stories such as woman, the tree, the snake. All were seen as material, sexual and earthly; these attributes would have been familiar to those conversant with the older culture as the attributes of the Goddess. The Priestly writers of Genesis show these qualities in a negative light with dire consequences. This crude piece of polemic has unfortunately worked well for Christian patriarchy. Perhaps the reason that it has lasted so long is that it was aided by the lens of Greek metaphysics through which it has been read for two thousand years.

This lens has meant that women have been blamed for being wicked but also it has brought about a split betwen the physical and spiritual realms. Life is understood as dualistic and the two human genders as complementary to each other. They are opposites, yet they complement each other; one cannot exist without the other, like the two sides of a coin.

> In this lies the root of women's inequality—for if males embody one set of characteristics, and if with characteristic modesty they arrogate to themselves all the strength and virtues, then women are necessarily opposite and lesser creatures; weak, where men are strong, fearful, where men are brave and stupid, where men are intelligent (Miles 1989: 100).

To this list we may add physical, where men are spiritual, emotional, where men are rational.

The biblical stories are 'myths' yet they have often been viewed as 'gospel truth'. This has meant that many people have been slow to deconstruct them. A feminist hermeneutic could see the Genesis story as one about seeking knowledge, not a story of 'original sin', which is a Christian and not a Jewish concept. Those who acknowledge the goddess background to the story understand that the goddess would encourage engagement with nature in the way that Eve did, to experience, to gain knowledge, to act. She would delight in their sensuous involvement with the tree, the fruit and the garden. This is, of course, far from the interpretation we have received and so we need to interpret it for ourselves. If there is a need to brand anything as 'original sin' we suggest it should be the murder of Abel, because it is the first story of a violent act committed by humans. This act signalled a rupture in human relationships and the destruction of mutuality. Christianity has chosen to overlook this breakdown in human relations as the fundamental sin of humanity and has instead focused on a narrow interpretation of the Genesis story whereby original sin is seen as the sin of sex.

The history of Israel, when it does refer to women, shows they had a secondary role in life. This is despite the fact that the rabbis did not interpret the Genesis myth in such a way as to place blame and guilt on women. They understood Genesis to show progress which would inevitably have mistakes within it; there is no mention of original sin. Nevertheless, women in the ancient world were in general thought of as chattels, either belonging to their father or husband or brother. They were held in low esteem, classed with slaves, children and the mentally ill. In the highly regulated world of ancient Israel women could not be witnesses in a law court because of their sex, they had no testicles upon which to swear (our words seminal and testimony/testament all springing from the ancient practice of holding the testicles when an oath was made or a truth spoken). Jewish women, with few exceptions such as Deborah, the judge, and Judith, the murderess, had no recognized function outside the family.

Men's activity was accepted or became accepted as the superior activity; production was primary, reproduction was secondary. Woman's role in reproduction was acknowledged as woman's contribution to the survival of the family, the clan, the ethnic group and mothers became very honoured, but also feared and persecuted as evil beings, 'witches', if they attempted to escape from this role to pursue an independent lifestyle. The function of woman was to be useful to man in some capacity. Women were seen as belonging to men, not fully human, objects without rights, a view which gained currency in almost all societies in antiquity. In general this view also shaped the attitudes of Christian societies of late antiquity.

The Radical Message?

It has been argued that the Christian message was something completely different. Christians have always tended to view it as radical, new and revelatory. Christian feminists have pointed to the actions of Jesus and claimed they gave new hope to women. They have argued that Jesus grasped God's commitment to compassion and his treatment of women was not normal for his day. He cured women, even when they were considered ritually unclean (Mt. 9.18-23), he spoke with women, even when they were from a despised race (Jn 4.5-26) and he offered women forgiveness, even if that meant challenging the law (Jn 9.1-11). Further, he defended women against criticism (Jn 12.1-9) and had them as close friends (Jn 11.1-4). The Christ was born to a woman (Lk. 2.1-8) and made his first resurrection appearance to a woman (Jn 20), who, significantly has in tradition been called a whore. Jesus' actions towards women do not suggest that he viewed them as insignificant. Despite all this he was said not to have women apostles and this has been used to justify an exclusively male ministry. The argument is that Jesus was so unusual in his treatment of women but still excluded them from the inner circle and so this must be as God wishes it. There are those who claim that he excluded women only out of expediency since the world of his day could not have accepted women apostles.

However, although rarely mentioned in the Gospels, women apostles are mentioned in the Acts as present with Mary at the birth of the Church at Pentecost. Women received the Holy Spirit equally with men and were prominent in the early Church. They were often Gentiles who actively spread the Good News from their own houses. Paul commended 'our sister Phoebe, a deaconess of the Church at Cenchreae', Prisca and her male co-worker Aquila 'my fellow workers in Christ Jesus... My greetings also to the Church that meets in their house'. Five other women workers are mentioned in the same passage, as is the convert Lydia, a business woman in Philippi (Rom. 16.1-5). Women went to meetings, they converted others, they actively promoted the gospel and they were publically thanked for it. Paul, of course, had preached the equality of all in Christ: 'For as many of you as were baptized into Christ, have put on Christ. There is neither Jew nor Greek, there is neither slave nor free, there is neither male nor female; for you are all one in Christ Jesus' (Gal. 3.27-28).

Recent scholarship (Mack 1993; Crossan 1992) makes it necessary for Christians to moderate the claims that they make about Jesus and therefore to look at his actions in a different light. We now know that there was a wide range of practices that could be called Jewish at the time of Jesus, some more conservative and others more liberal than that which Jesus followed. Indeed, a picture of a rather eclectic religion emerges from the pages of the Gospels, one that can not be fully identified with any existing form of practice but one that reflects many. It does appear to be true that Jesus championed those on the margins and looked towards a time when equality would be more evident. However, in a world where a small number of women did lead synagogues and have ownership of businesses we can hardly claim his treatment of them was radical. It has long been pointed out by Jewish feminists that Christian feminists tend to portray Jesus as the saviour of otherwise poor and downtrodden women. This they find insulting as a record that is not entirely accurate and they urge a more critical eye from Christain feminist scholars.

This critical eye has been applied by feminists for a long time to Paul and so more critique of him will not be a surprise. However, it is rather disheartening to realize that even the Gal. 3.27-28 passage may not be what it appears to be. At first glance it is a passage about radical equality, on closer inspection we see that women are assumed to disappear in the original and glorious creation which is man (Børreson 1995: 62). The wayward rib slots neatly back into place and the rupture in creation is overcome. While Paul is not Jesus and the church he nurtured is not the Jesus movement we have to be alarmed that so early in the day women are being written out. As we know this has been a recurring pattern in Christian theology and religious practice.

We have then a very mixed early heritage, far more than we ever imagined. The question of whether it is useable for Christian feminists remains an urgent one and one that exercises the minds of many of our best scholars. There is hope if we remember that what we view as orthodox teaching has taken a long time to emerge and is more to do with politics than it is to do with divine revelation. The Christ we have handed to us as the one who is the same throughout all time can be demonstrated to have changed, that is in our perceptions. For example, the ideas of Arius have at times been in favour and at others not. It is this more realistic and flexible understanding of the development of the Christian message that acts as the greatest spur for those who wish to develop it still further—Christian feminists. Jesus was not a feminist but he was on the side of the marginalized and oppressed. In the world in which we live where the global reality of women is dire, Christians are also called to be feminists, to fight for the dignity and rights of women and all the marginalized.

The Reduction of the Message

Despite the encouraging, if not radical, start that early Christianity made the situation of women seemed to decline rapidly. There is the famous injunction for women to remain silent at meetings (1 Cor. 14.34-35):

> As in all the churches of the saints, the women should keep silence in the churches. For they are not permitted to speak, but should be subordinate, as even the law says. If there is anything they desire to know, let them ask their husbands at home. For it is shameful for a woman to speak in church.

What all this indicates is that women had obviously not kept quiet at meetings, had asked questions and had not kept in the background. Whether their questions were difficult for the men to answer or whether women actually questioned the creeping restrictions upon the freedom originally granted to them in baptism, the fact was that the charismatic freedom of the early church was eroded quite quickly (cf. Wire 1995).

One reason for this was Paul's negative attitude towards sex (for example, 1 Cor. 6.18) which had terrible consequences for women. His lack of enthusiasm for sexual relationships was due to his sense of living in the 'end-time'. Christ was believed to be returning soon and so Paul felt it best to spend time preparing for this by spiritual pursuits rather than by becoming involved in sexual relationships. Therefore, his negative attitudes to sex should be understood in this context, simply as a short term measure. Sadly, the Church Fathers who lived in quite different times took his words and used them to back up their own sexual neuroses (Brown 1989).

Faith of our Fathers

We see as early as 100 CE through an examination of Clement of Rome that there was a concerted effort to restrict the role of women. This was done by moving worship from houses, where women were very much in evidence as presiders, to buildings that were formerly used as ritual places where local deities were worshipped. Along with this went the passing of all ministerial roles from men to women. In the end there was only an order of widows left whose role was greatly confined (see Fiorenza 1983; Torjesen 1995). Gradually the Christian communities grew and the underground movement emerged triumphantly under the Emperor Constantine. It was no longer a sect set in Jewish culture, but firmly rooted in Graeco-Roman culture. Thus, the position of woman was not equal with that of man, but subservient. While the order of widows was continued it is also likely that there were deacons. They were allowed to engage in charitable works, but forbidden to undertake religious instruction or administer the sacraments. The Syrian *Didascalia*, a book of church order from the early third century, mentions this prohibition, which implies that widows had been accustomed to serve in this capacity.

Further, as Jesus failed to return, the church became more concerned with the world and so was more open to its prejudices and preoccupations. The world of the Roman empire, permeated with numerous religious traditions alongside the emperor cult, was deeply misogynistic. The many ascetic sects were a reaction to the excesses they believed had brought about the decline of the Roman world. Christianity was inevitably effected by these movements. This reinforced the notion that the material, the physical, led to decline and this same notion was again tragic news for women.

The diaconate, the presbyterial and episcopal offices had developed into male preserves. Women must have fought this—the Council of Laodicea in 343 decreed that women might not be appointed as elders or presbyterae in the church. As we know from a fresco in the Catacomb of Priscilla in Rome, women were concelebrating the Eucharist as a matter of course, in this instance a group of virgins living together.

By the fourth century the church had thoroughly undermined the way in which women had initially taken a large part in its life and ministry. Women however, attempted to take seriously the baptismal promises of equality by looking for ways of life that were not so restricted. It has been suggested that many women took inspiration for life beyond the bounds of the norms of antiquity from the apocryphal gospels, some of which had been written by women (McNamara 1985). Given the constraints of their societies they had to look for this freedom away from the home and in communities. There they were able to develop autonomy and exercise their talents. Far from being a place that women fled to under the weight of assumptions about the evils of the flesh, it seems that these communities of women were originally set up as a celebration of baptismal equality and in the face of a sexist church. Even this caused problems for male clergy. Tertullian and the African churches debated long and hard as to whether these women had become allegorical males and could therefore exercise male roles in the church (McNamara 1985: 78). What is clear from that debate is that women, as themselves, could no longer be seen as exercising roles of authority and leadership. It was obviously less absurd to see them as allegorical males than to see them as leaders. Despite these debates and efforts to contain women's communities, their existence and the celibate life that went with them enabled women to live a life against male definitions and reject sexual stereotyping for quite some time.

Theologians like Augustine witnessed the fall of Rome to the barbarian Vandals and Goths, the uncivilized invaders, who had obliterated Roman sophistication. It is little wonder that he believed rational self-control was necessary, if man was not to be dragged into decline. Christians were suffering from anxiety because Jesus had not returned and the world was crumbling. They began to view the world as a place where one did battle with the body in order to preserve the soul. The fourth-century bishop Ambrose was able to write 'Think of the soul rising free of the body having turned away from sexuality and the sweet pleasures of the flesh, and cast off the cares of this worldly life' (*Isaac* 3.18). Augustine was able to claim that before the Fall sex was rational and not pleasurable but due to Eve it became passionate and pleasurable and this encouraged people to forget God. Once again, Eve takes the blame and sin, sex and women are bound ever tighter together in an unholy triple alliance.

The physical and therefore sinful nature of women was further emphasized by the insistence on the virginity of Mary. A woman who was looking for a way out, going beyond the role allotted to her by society's view of her biology, could model herself on saints who were usually celibate and often virgins. Karen Armstrong deals extensively with the negative aspects for women of this cult of virgins and martyr saints in her book *The Gospel According to Woman* (1986). The main point is that if women were willing to deny their sexuality, they could gain some status, and further, if they were willing to undergo torture, whether self inflicted or inflicted by others, they could receive martyrdom, and thus in some measure overcome their 'Eve-natures'. How different this is from some women's early views of celibacy. The idea was still prevalent that they could cease to be woman and would become man. 'As long as a woman is for children she is different from man as body is from soul. But when she wishes to serve Christ more than the world, then she will cease to be a woman and will be called man' (Jerome, *Comm. Eph.* 3.5). A remnant of this idea has survived until recently in the custom of giving women wishing to become nuns male first names.

The spiritual directors of these women, who were men, encouraged all kinds of body negating practices from starvation (fasting) to mutilation. Catherine of Siena displays all the symptoms of the modern day anorexic, but she was not treated for her illness, rather she was lauded for it. Her directors and contemporaries regarded her as a walking miracle, but her holiness seemed to lie in her devotion to a living death. Catherine did allow herself to drink liquid, 'the water in which she had washed a cancerous wound' (Armstrong 1986: 154). Her confessors and directors never attempted to dissuade her from any of her practices since they were seen to be negation of the body, in this case the female body. Their behaviour was not motivated by medical ignorance, but rather by the belief that the body had to be controlled by punishment and negation. Margaret Mary Alacoque is a sad example of masochistic violence, yet to the church she is a fine example of catholic womanhood. In 1675 she received the vision of the Sacred Heart, Jesus' exposed bleeding heart, and the privilege of drinking from it. She bound her body tightly with cords full of knots so that she could neither breathe nor eat. When she removed the knotted cord, she also removed lumps of flesh. The open sores often became ulcerous. This gave her great delight (Armstrong 1986: 162).

Once these women excelled in such activities and accepted total annihilation of the self—martyrdom—they were called saints by the male hierarchy. Christian history is littered with such victims who have been placed before women as ideal role models. The picture emerges that the truly Christian woman is self sacrificing and set firmly on the path of self-annihilation. What a shame that women have not, until recently, had sight of the other story, that of women questioning their lack of equality and seekings alternate ways of life.

It was tragic that the views of the Church Fathers from the fourth and fifth centuries continued clerical thinking on the fallen nature of woman. Convinced of her inferiority they confined her to two lifestyles: she could be a wife or a mother, or she could choose consecrated virginity in a cloistered community. If the latter, she must rise above her female nature and become spiritually male. Jerome, Ambrose, Tertullian, Clement of Alexandria, Cyril of Alexandria, John Damascene displayed considerable hostility to women; the language they employed was not just culturally conditioned misogyny but vicious ridicule and obscene stereotype. Tertullian's dictum: 'Woman, you are the devil's gateway. You have led astray one whom the devil would not dare attack directly. It is your fault that the Son of God had to die; you should always go in mourning and in rags... You destroyed so easily God's image, man'

(Armstrong 1986: 55) and St John Chrysostom's words: 'Among all savage beasts none is found so harmful as woman' (quoted in Beauvoir 1988: 129) stand here for a whole host of sayings about and against women which heap guilt on women. The scapegoat syndrome, the need to blame somebody for all ills, reveals a deep-seated disease in the writers.

Augustine can only believe that the redemption of women occurs in some secondary fashion, while Aquinas cannot understand why God created this 'misbegotten male'. He adopted many of the Church Fathers' judgments on women and all of it was based on very faulty physiology. Aquinas held that women would not have been created at all had they not been required for the service of men and that they were only conceived when a damp south wind was blowing (cf. Ranke-Heinemann 1990). Woman is nothing more than the matter in which the fully formed human is implanted by the 'divine sperm' (Aquinas, *ST*, I, q.92, a.1), she is therefore useful but nevertheless dangerous.

There is a growing body of work on the topic of women and redemption (Ruether 1998) and it is sobering to see that it is a relatively new idea, perhaps as late as eighteenth century, that women and men are truly equal in the matter of redemption: Women do not have to become different in order to 'qualify' for redemption. At best this meant a spiritualization of notions of redemption that did little to change the unequal realities of women's lives. At worst we hear Church Fathers musing over the nature of the resurrected woman and concluding that she would be part man and part angel, obliterated for salvation.

Women's Choice?

In the Middle Ages the church provided the opportunity for women to leave home and live a cloistered unmarried life. Abbesses, very often royal women, especially in the early mediaeval period, ruled over vast estates and were endowed with all the feudal rights that went with them. They were autonomous; they even had monasteries of men within their jurisdiction and seem to have ordained them. They certainly administered other sacraments. But here as well, with the progressive acceptance of Roman law, local law was pushed back and local custom eradicated (Valerio 1991; Sawyer 1987).

Both families and church authorities tried to control women and tried to censure their moves. In the thirteenth century, the Beguines, a group of women living in communities, fought the imposition of priests as their superiors but eventually had to give in. They chose a life outside marriage at a time when the church had made marriage a sacrament, 'yet had forbidden it to the Christian elite', referring to the ban on married priests (Beauvoir 1988: 136). The view that women were created for marriage, but were not allowed to marry priests, or, in the case of the Beguines, were not allowed to live without clerical domination, again shows the contradiction inherent in a church based on Jesus' teaching of inclusivity and its negation by the hierarchy. Against this background it is not surprising that women's role in the church was progressively reduced.

What did women themselves have to say about these prescriptions concerning their conduct and function? The means of resisting were very limited; they were less educated than men and they were economically dependent on men. But there were women who were educated, who worked as pharmacists and teachers, as craftswomen and artists and who lived by their profession (Fox 1990). They did not tolerate being dictated to by clergy who were often less educated than they were. Christine de Pisan (1363–about 1431) was widowed with three children at the age of 25 and kept herself by writing. In 1402 she defended her own sex in a spirited attack, maintaining that with the benefit of education girls would be as capable as boys (Pisan 1982).

In the sixteenth century, many women must have hoped for a redefinition of their status when the German clergy openly defied Roman law. Foremost amongst the hopeful women must have been the so-called 'concubines, the 'priest whores', the women, who lived and worked with their priest husbands and were not acknowledged as their wives. Priests paid annual fines to the episcopal coffers for the privilege of living with a woman despite their vow of celibacy (McEwan 1987). Luther, who fought against the creeping Romanization in the Catholic church, did not fight to improve the lot of women. The only right for women was to be silent in church and to follow the role model of pious obedient wife and mother. The emphasis on female purity and its converse female pollution was a way of controlling women and keeping power in the hands of the men. Luther said 'A woman is never truly her own master. God formed her body to belong to a man, to have and to rear children' (Luther 1933: 327). The first part of this statement was recognized in British Law until 1991 when marital rape was declared a criminal offence. Until then it was assumed that men owned the bodies of their wives. A respectable woman was a married woman who had many children. Even if a woman was not married and earned her living by prostitution in Reformation Germany, she was placed under the supervision of a man, the town's henchman who was paid for by taxing the prostitutes (Roper 1991: 89).

Luther further shows his contempt for women by declaring 'Let them bear children till they die of it. That is what they are for' (Luther 1933: 328). Woman is still Eve and sex in marriage is still dangerous but God 'will wink at it'. Within the family set-up man, being more rational and in the likeness of God, can have total control, while woman is kept dependent. All kinds of abuse of women was acceptable under the protection of marriage vows. Indeed, Canon Law even allowed men to beat their wives with a stick as long as the stick was no thicker than a finger. A husband was supposed to chastise his wife moderately unless he was a cleric, in which case he had to increase her punishment (Borrowdale 1991: 104).

No Further!

This general contempt for women persisted in the churches into the nineteenth century. No wonder that women under the influence of other factors in society started to organize in order to change secular laws such as the Married Women's Property Acts, the law enabling women to study at universities and the franchise laws. The first wave of modern feminism originated in the abolition of slavery movement. It is no coincidence that a woman who was active on the hustings in the anti-racist debates turned her attention to the role religion played in justifying the secondary status of women. In 1895, the octogenarian Elisabeth Cady Stanton published *The Woman's Bible*, an exegetical work in which all anti-feminist passages were cut out. She was severely criticized for it and completely misunderstood, for what she wanted to do was to highlight the fact that women figure only marginally in the most important religious texts in Christianity. The significance of her contributions lies in the fact, that she started the long overdue process of biblical interpretation by and for women. Today biblical scholars do not support her method, but she must be given credit for triggering a process which led to brilliant scholarly research by other women (Elizabeth Schüssler Fiorenza, Rosemary Radford Ruether among many others.)

Women come through in this analysis as survivors, having survived the 'roles of servant, slave, institutional "sufferer". They have survived as long-suffering mother, silent sister, dutiful daughter, uncomplaining domestic worker. They have survived their silence, their humility, their subservience. They have even survived their own church history which, until now, has largely been a legacy of anonymity' (Ohanneson 1980: 137). Women's experiences of oppression appear systemic in every culture.

While certain advances have been made in the secular world the churches have lagged behind development in society. Despite the churches of the Anglican communion ordaining women to the priesthood and Episcopal office there seems to be little change in the way women are viewed. Further, the Catholic church, becalmed for centuries and only refloated when Pope John XXIII launched the Second Vatican Council in the 1960s, has issued a document which expressly declares 'Every type of discrimination based on sex is to be overcome and eradicated as contrary to God's intent' (*Gaudium et Spes*, 29). Great words but no action. The debate for the ordination of Catholic women still finds itself beset with notions of the inability of women to represent Christ and the inability of popes to change matters of revealed doctrine. How can the church still believe this is in the face of the facts. The church has always changed things and rightly so. There is an increasing mood in the Catholic church which at worst equates feminism with the anti-Christ and at best thinks that too much fuss is being made about nothing.

Despite some advances women are still not allowed to forget the Eve trap. The Church of England former bishop of London, Dr Graham Leonard, argued against the ordination of women not only because he sees it as non-biblical, but because a woman at the altar would lead men into sin; she would cause them to wish to embrace her which would be a sin. His argument sounds quite like those used to acquit the defendant in rape cases. Members of MOW (The Movement for the Ordination of Women) were horrified to be greeted with cries of 'Keep the whores out of the temple' when they kept a vigil outside the Lambeth conference in 1989. Those shouting were male clergy. The Prefect of the Congregation of Faith, Cardinal Joseph Ratzinger, said in an interview with the respected German weekly *Die Zeit* in the context of a discussion on artificial versus natural birth control, that 'priority must given to the fact that sexuality will be led from its mere animal aspect to the human aspect, to the community of love, out of which all human future is created only through the practice of natural birth control'.[1] The unholy trinity of woman, sex and sin is still not very far from the surface in the male mind. Unfortunately this has been brought to the fore with an increasing number of women ministers/priests reporting sexual abuse by male colleagues and parishioners. Amongst the first to report this were American Methodist ministers, who noted that home visits were becoming increasingly difficult and that some men on parish committees tended to treat them in inappropriate ways, reminding them that their jobs depended on keeping the men sweet. This kind of 'reminding' has always in our societies carried an unspoken assumption that there is a price to pay and women have often been required to pay with their bodies.

While the position for women ministers and priests is at times grave, the position of those in the academy is not always better. It is still a battle to have feminist scholarship recognized and included in most academic subjects. The inclusion is often an afterthought and many male academics do not even bother to acknowledge the work of women in the field. At the turn of the century it is still more than possible to open academic books written by men and find no woman in the bibliography, let alone a feminist scholar. However, feminist scholars are often criticized for not mentioning in depth the work of some male scholars. The assumed male possession of texts continues and the word is still understood as male.

Patriarchal theology still encourages women to see themselves in the Eve trap, as different, deviant and therefore not quite equal. What women have to say, how they say it and the actions that follow from their thoughts and words are still viewed as off the mark. They are often tolerated but never mainstreamed. This is a frustrating situation for women who know that their voices are never really heard; therefore we address the words of Jesus to such theology, religion and organizations: 'This people honours with their lips, but their heart is far from me; in vain do they worship me, teaching as doctrines the precepts of men'... You leave the commandment of God and hold fast the tradition of men' (Mk 7.6-8).

1.   *Die Zeit*, No. 49 (29 November 1991): 22.

Chapter 3

Mary: Empowered Womanhood or Archetypal Victim?

When Mary gives voice to the Magnificat (Lk. 1.46-55) announcing 'from this day forward all generations will call me blessed' (Lk. 1.48), a revolution is proclaimed, one in which the lowly handmaid is raised up by the power of God. The Magnificat is based on the song of Hannah (1 Sam. 2.1-10) and originally described God's favour towards Israel and especially towards the poor and lowly. Could this signal a turning point for women? Here we are told woman was giving birth to divinity. Was it really to be a revolution for women?

Very little of the historical Mary is known; she was a Jewish wife and mother following the religious rules laid upon woman of her time in history. Because of lack of scriptural evidence the Christian inter-pretation of her had recourse to inspiration by the Holy Spirit, loading her image with exemplary chastity and humility, which in turn was interpreted as submissiveness. Mary as a role model is a contradictory one, which cannot be followed by a single woman: As women we can be either one or other, but never a virgin and a mother and yet this is precisely what the church teaches about Mary. What is more, the pic-torial images we associate with Mary, the teenage mother holding the child Jesus on her arm, and Mary, the older mother, holding the corpse of her dead son Jesus on her lap, are two positives that denote respec-tively joy and grief, both archetypal human experiences. They do not tell us more beyond these two experiences, they do not tell us anything of Mary, the woman.

So how did the physical mother of a baby son become a non-sexual role model for women? The cultural fusion of Jewish views regarding women as second-class with Graeco-Roman views of late antiquity that still reflected the misogyny of classical Greece, narrowed the options for women in society. Women's sexuality was equated with women's nature, women were only narrowly valued for their biological roles as mothers and nurturers.

The Church Fathers, faced with the dilemma of how to deal with Mary's femaleness, declared Mary 'ever virgin', thereby elevating her above all other women and defining virginity a more elevated state than motherhood. They used strong language full of contempt for women, but through the declaration of the perpetual virginity of the Mother of God (itself a very difficult concept: how can God, the creator, have a mother from whom he is created?), the fathers embarked on a road of declaring fantasy as fact and of siting 'facts' which are patently impossible, in the realm of 'mysteries'. The subject of sexuality, held in scorn, was dealt with in a swift act of theological mutilation and in the teaching on Mary it atrophied even further and became a negative influence for women. She is not a model that empowers women through their sexuality, but rather a model that encourages the repression and denial of women's sexuality and once again emphasizes the negative aspect of women's natures.

By exalting Mary to the icon of the Mother of God, the common bond of humanity between Mary and humankind is cut. Mary is the symbol and instrument of dualistic thinking: if Mary is perfect, then we are not; if Mary is ever-pure, then we are not; if Mary is goodness personified, then we are not. All this serves to underpin women's subjection to their biology; women are not 'pure', they are defiled by the sex act—something to which Mary never had to submit. That Mary had other children is still fiercely denied by many exponents of patriarchal theology.

All this serves to underpin that women are subject to physiological determinants making them second-class citizens. Mary was placed so far above real women as to be treated as an ideal of perfection unattainable by ordinary women, thus increasing, not diminishing, their feelings of inferiority. It is precisely this exalted position projected onto Mary that needs to be reinterpreted by women and *not for* women, otherwise the teaching on Mary is mere Mariolatry. In history Mary has been invested with a host of roles, but could a 'mere woman' ever aspire to match the qualities of the Virgin Mother of God? When 'knightly love' appeared in the twelfth century in the feudal houses of mediaeval Europe, it was modelled on the one licit worship of woman, the cult of the Virgin. The young man in love with his 'Dame' could not write or sing of her in ordinary language to show how noble she was, far above other women. He addressed her as Mary, the celestial noble chatelaine, 'Our Lady', the female castellan, beyond reproach, all-just and all powerful. By invoking Mary's unimpeachable goodness and beauty, the young man thinly disguised his worship and passion for his love as worship and passion for Mary. But what about the woman? She must have felt herself unworthy of such praise precisely because she was not all-powerful. For her, the cult of the Virgin and the mother of the Redeemer offered a role model she found impossible to follow. And yet the church exalted it in the twelfth and thirteenth centuries to such a degree that Beauvoir is prompted to call this idolatrous worship of Mary: 'God had been made woman' (Beauvoir 1988: 131).

It did not do much for the status of women, but it could be argued that the women's religious orders based on the 'ideal' of virginity gave women some degree of autonomy. This is certainly true, but only for a very small number of women. Still, to enter cloistered life was the one respectable way for a woman to withdraw from family responsibilities.

The Mary of the Gospels, the Mary in the Apocrypha, became the model for dealing with absolutely every situation in one's life. Her titles, Second Eve, Queen of Heaven, Madonna, Milk of Paradise, Mater Dolorosa, The Immaculate Conception, to quote but a few, offer a bewildering selection of values. Mary has huge responsibilities! The male hierarchy again and again exhorts us to 'flee' to Mary's powers of intercession, to Mary as the most sublime and beautiful woman doing God's will. Why? Because Mary triumphed over weakness and evil, humanity and sex. The doctrine of the virgin birth, an ancient concept of the power of the deity found with many Middle Eastern and African cultures, led, in Christianity, to an emphasis on the values of virginity, from sign to doctrine, that 'transformed the mother goddess of antiquity into an effective instrument of female subjection' (Warner 1976: 67).

As mother, Mary sanctifies procreation, but as virgin mother she gives a confused message about the institution for procreation, marriage, the value put on motherhood and, in parenthesis, the injunction on abortion, has sentenced women over the centuries to multiple pregnancies which valued life in the womb and the child over the mother. The RC Church still holds that a women who has been raped has no right to terminate the pregnancy. There are many medical, physical and mental consequences of following the obedient Mary.

The cult of Mary, usually widespread in societies where the position of women is low, is in our view a continuation and perpetuation of the ancient cult of motherhood, because Mary is accepted by many more women as a model for motherhood than for virginity. The cult is often found in poor countries where the economic implications of repeated pregnancies are devastating. Mary does not appear very empowering in this situation. In Catholic Christianity, marriage, a relationship in partnership, is rated a poor second to virginity and chastity. Celibacy, that is compulsory chastity as decreed for priests in the RC Church, springs from the same interpretation, that relationships defile and that the unmarried state is intrinsically better than the married one. The need to reinterpret positions, which are arrived at speculatively and emotionally, holds true for both the cult of Mary and priestly celibacy.

The churches have therefore paid little attention to helping people develop equal and mutually respecting partnerships. Indeed, pastors find themselves able to tell women 'Each time your husbands hits you, think of it as an opportunity to be closer to Jesus' (Borrowdale 1991: 104) and church leaders make no comment when judges declare that marital rape is not serious (1991: 105). After a long legal battle marital rape is now a crime in the courts of Britain. Slowly the churches are beginning to address domestic violence although there is still a view that it is not prevalent in Christian families.

The feminist theologian Mary Daly, a 'post-Christian', sees nothing positive in the image of Mary for women. For her it symbolizes the total erasing of Mary's self. She is the archetypal rape victim who sets the pattern for all women (Daly 1987: 85). A terrified young girl is confronted by an angel who does not ask her, but tells her she will bear a son. Daly says it was not necessary to depict physical rape, as some other early patriarchal rapes (e.g. Persephone) of the Goddess do, since Mary's reply 'be it done to me according to thy word' signifies that her mind/ will/ spirit has already been invaded. Daly says 'within the rapist Christian myth of the Virgin Birth the role of Mary is utterly minimal; yet she is there' (1987: 85). She does not query or offer any counter arguments, she simply gives herself away.

She is passive and obedient; she seeks nothing but to serve. She is going to give birth to the son of God but she does not seek power; she accepts her fate as dictated by others. Daly claims Mary's annihilation is taken back even before her birth by the doctrine of the Immaculate Conception. Mary, even before her own birth, was pure and without sin. What kind of image is this? It is one of a woman who has no power over her own life—by divine decree.

The private sphere, the paradigmatic woman's sphere, was not created by women; women were assigned to it, backed up with divine commands and public legislation. Any woman seeking power was accused of taking on male character traits and of stepping out of her God-ordained station. Mary, of course, was not seeking power or any other role. Therefore, she cannot function as a true role model to women who want to do just that, to step out of an allotted role because they argue it is thwarting their creativity and curtailing their talents. Women today seek both personal power to run their own lives and corporate strength to engage with other men and women in improving their lot. Mary as a passive icon of obedience can no longer function as role model, women want to take their talents and creativity seriously.

The difficulties are all around, in the huge task of building up individual self confidence and self determination, self value and self assertiveness, but even more so, in seeking to press as a group to combat the sexism pervading society, whether in its crass forms of wife beating, incest, rape and pornography or in the less crass but more sweeping forms of women being abused by ridicule, groping and suggestive language. It is clear that many women find the task too daunting; they are up against peers, subordinates, superiors on the job; they are inexperienced in claiming their rights publically and they just turn a blind eye and collude. They do not want to be a 'bad sport' and so internalize their suffering in silence. They find it very difficult to resist patriarchal patterns of authority.

Today there is growing resentment at the harm being done to women in the name of Christianity when Mary is held up as the role model, for women are told that any suffering is natural and that their 'meek and mild' acceptance of all the world throws at them is holy and reflects the example of the Virgin. Mary must be 'dis-endowed' from all the stereotypes and attributes cluttering up a healthy understanding of her role. We are sure, Mary is 'quite contrary' to all those attributes. As a mother, whose son is sentenced and executed, many women who share her fate, can empathize with her. As an exalted virgin-mother it is very difficult for her to mean anything to women. Patriarchy has made Mary a victim; it is part of the task of feminist theology to empower her once again by seeing her as the unmarried mother who through courage brought divinity to birth.

There is some move towards this view amongst the women of Asia who understand the virginity of Mary as a relational reality. That is to say she is a liberated individual who is not subject to any other human being. Virginity then is understood as the ability to be self defining and is not to do with whether one is sexually active or not. It is a process that women can reach through life experience and a growing awareness of their self worth. Women become people in their own right and not in relation to husbands, children or fathers. The virginity of Mary comes to symbolize the overturning of the patriarchal order and a sign that full and liberated womanhood is possible (Chung 1991: 79).

PART II

Chapter 4

Method in Feminist Theology

If equality is to be advanced the task is twofold. First, the structures that inhibit equality have to be identified, singled out and named and then positive steps have to be taken to devise and promote strategies that enhance equality. Feminism with its agenda of justice making is the way out of the inequality, that is the consequence of age-old dualistic thinking. Social interactions must cease which, on the one hand, push women to the margins, and on the other hand, raise women to the status of the model of morality. The absurdity and injustice of such a situation have to be brought to the attention of those who perpetuate it. In the field of theology and religion this will mean that women's awareness of themselves will reawaken an awareness of female aspects of the divine that have so far been obliterated. We have to look at the biblical affirmation of women (Swidler 1979), at the way women have survived the oppressive church dictates and mandates, and are surfacing beyond the stories of the Fall and stories of impurity consequent upon it.

Feminist theology offers a different approach to the religious understanding of women and men by exposing the cultural conditioning of religious belief. This involves for some a re-examination of religious tenets, a re-think and a re-appraisal of whether traditional forms of worship are meaningful or meaningless. For others it is a discipline in search of truth, understanding that the past can only be experienced through seeing how relations in the present are constituted. Truth can only be discovered through the experience of its meaning within the lives of the people, not through the authoritative pronouncements of officials in power.

When experience becomes the criterion of authority, old structures no longer fit. Women who felt they could no longer worship in their parish setting or keep their faith alive in isolation, sparked 'woman church'. In an informal setting, women can feel spiritually at home, they are no longer second-class citizens, no longer strangers, no longer competitors, no longer subject women or 'beloved brethren'. The term 'Woman church' has been used to describe groups of people coming together for worship. It may sometimes be exclusively for women, sometimes for women and men together. It may have a fixed pattern of worship or a very flexible one. It may experiment with the use of rituals and language so as to accommodate the spiritual needs of everybody assembled. It is not an organization, but a method, not a structure, but a space and time filled by the agenda of inclusiveness and equality. Being together becomes being. This entails decisions on appropriate ways of expressing women's spirituality. Women's input in church life and religion is not exhausted by flower arranging or charity work. While these are choices for some, they are not gender-dictated absolutes for all.

Religion is not about standing still, repeating established 'truths', being limited by accepted interpretations; religion is about the communion of community in the present, the interrelatedness of everybody, connecting and networking, carrying and caring. Thus feminist theology presents a radical critique of religious and theological thinking stuck in notions of patriarchal supremacy.

The task of this critique is as follows:

- to identify what is oppressive to women and men in the present practice of theology and its interpretation;
- to recognize that self-reliant and local and endogenous interpretations provide the spiritual sustenance women and men need from religion;
- to share a vision of a just and participatory system geared to local needs;
- to provide effective ways of mass participation;
- to empower women and men to become agents in creating a more just society;
- to acknowledge that the increments gained in participation, knowledge and vitality in the new communities must not be attained at the cost of somebody else.

Many traditional religious leaders would argue that feminism seeks to separate women from the churches. Women certainly have no wish to be coopted any longer into structures that are still oppressive to women. 'Working for change within the structure which draws its strength from our subjugation verges on the futile, and is damaging to ourselves' (Webster 1991). Women are not engaged simply in reforming bad structures. Bad structures, like apartheid, have to be destroyed. But women are interested in transforming structures, in being church, in being in the church as equal partners with men.

Jesus sparked a movement of people who, trusting in God, were told to ignore all barriers among themselves and level out the differences in power and possessions. Such guidelines should regulate the interaction of people, should overcome fear of the people and the strategy of colluding with the powers that be. Many religious and political leaders do not accept or understand the withholding assent or refusal of guilt-tripping stance that women have taken, they do not grasp that we no longer support structures abusive to women and men. This entails a learning process for those in power, who feel they have to have the last word. It is a dominant delusion, since they can no longer subjugate knowledge.

Feminism as a critique of society points to the gap between the potential and its actualization; precisely because of this gap it meets with much psychological resistance. And yet, a cross-section of society is increasingly interested in and influenced by feminism, and significantly so by feminist theology. Women have traditionally been excluded from the hierarchy within church structures and have found it increasingly difficult to understand that the message as conveyed by that male hierarchy was 'good news' for them. But now that women have become theologically literate, they are no longer dependent on somebody else for exegesis and can therefore contribute to the vital discussion of theology from our understanding of life experience.

It means realizing that women have a right to pose questions and formulate answers. This realization in turn becomes a very powerful method and tool to be employed against overpowering structures, because individuals are attempting to retain their identity.

The Process of Liberation

The insights of first wave feminism did not effect or influence patriarchal theology; the main response from clergy was to restate the place of women—a very traditional place. Some women made attempts to influence the theological structures by pointing out their racist and sexist content, feminists were reflecting and questioning, but what we now know as feminist theology was not on the agenda. Women made their theological reflections felt through social practice—questioning the view of society on reproductive rights, on prostitution, on suffrage, on access to employment and education and so on—but the academic realm remained untouched, indeed almost untouchable.

A breakthrough came with two major contributions to the theological field this century that have allowed women to legitimate their experience as forms of theological reflection: Process Thought and Liberation Theology. In order to bring the methodologies and basic tenets of these modes of thought into focus it is important to set them against the background of the prevailing thought system in Europe. Our culture has been greatly influenced by the French thinker René Descartes who encouraged people to believe that their worth lay in their rational, thinking ability: 'I think therefore I am'. Thus 'thinking', the stress on rational thought is viewed not only as separate from, but indeed superior to the physical part of our nature. Our physical nature is seen as akin to the animal world. What separates us from it is our intellect, which makes us the pinnacle of creation. This thought dualism, body: mind perpetuates the old medieval and pre-Christian Greek division of the world into good and bad, black and white, body and mind. The mind was interpreted as belonging to the transcendent realm of spirit, the body did not belong to this realm since it resides in an inferior realm and needs to be subdued and controlled. If it is not controlled it can cause the degeneration of the mind, which brings about moral chaos or put another way, surrender to the passions. The generally accepted way of dealing with this was to strive to be a disembodied being—to raise the mind (spirit) above the realm of nature and body (cf. Plato, *Phaedrus* 246 –249).

In Greek thought women are associated with body and men with mind. In Aristotle we read that ruling-class Greek males exemplify mind (spirit) while women, slaves and barbarians are naturally servile since they represent the passions that need to be ruled by the 'head' (Aristotle, *Politics* 1.5). This dualistic interpretation does not stop there; it becomes a value judgment and inevitably a hierarchy:

God

    Spirits

        Male

            Female

                Non human Nature

It also becomes a chain of command, and the further one is from nature—from feeling—the nearer one is to perfection (God). Descartes, to some degree, echoes this by viewing 'substance' as that which needs nothing but itself to exist, with God being the pinnacle of this kind of substance, totally removed and self contained in some kind of cerebral existence.

Under the weight of this intellectual history the West from the period of Enlightenment in the eighteenth century onward has developed a rational world, split into 'subjects' and 'objects', with humanity and God regarded as above and beyond 'nature' and 'culture'. Our societies reflect this division as it 'aids' or clarifies separation in many respects and psychologies even declare that separation is a sign of maturity. Significantly in psychological testing, women fail to reach many of the levels that signal this kind of 'maturity'. Carol Gilligan showed that in consequence women are then termed immature, not fully human beings. The tests themselves have rarely been questioned until recently (Gilligan 1982), when women started to do just that to find a way out of this world view of pairs of dualisms. As long as societies and churches regard dualism as central to their philosophy they will pursue antagonistic policies and exclusive theologies. But who stands at the heart of Christian theology? Aristotle and his philosophy of dualisms or Jesus and his teaching of overcoming them in inclusivity? The introduction of Process Thought to Western thinking has been a step beyond dualisms in many disciplines, not least theology.

Process Thought

The founder of Process Thought in its generally accepted form was Alfred North Whitehead, who was by training a mathematician and theoretical physicist. Although these were his formal academic areas, his interests and the scope of his reading went far beyond. His wife was a major influence in broadening his horizons to encompass the humanities, art and particularly music. He says it was she who made him understand that an awareness of beauty of form, sound and colour is the centre of a truly human experience. The process perspective itself invites us to take these enjoyments and recognize their importance as it is concerned with analysing human experience at its most profound. Process Thought, however goes beyond looking at experience abstractly and tries to get to the heart of what it is like to be human.

Through research in many and varied disciplines it became clear, towards the end of the nineteenth century, that the world we inhabit is the product of an evolutionary process. In Britain thinkers like Samuel Alexander, Conway Lloyd-Morgan and Jan Smuts began in the early twentieth century to work out a general philosophy that took seriously the total dynamic and evolutionary perspectives of these research findings. They insisted on the relational and interpenetrative nature of the world. Whitehead did not like referring to the ideas as a system but rather as a 'vision of reality' and part of that reality for him was the undeniable fact that our world is one of relationships. Therefore the world is not dualistic, but relational, everything is in relation to everything else. From this understanding he concluded that the aim of life was not to develop objective thought but empathetic feeling (Whitehead 1929).

In his work *Modes of Thought* Whitehead takes a leap of imagination from physics to a 'vision of reality'. To him energy and the energetic activity observable in the world through the study of physics is in fact the 'emotional intensity entertained in life' (Whitehead 1929: 232). This then produces an intimate linkage between the thrust of human existence towards the achievement of goals and the creative movement of the cosmic order in its evolutionary drive. Life is part of the cosmic process of evolution and so this process is disclosed in some fashion in human experience. The world, the created universe is given concrete and particular expression in our own vital existence. We partake in the creative process and really understand our true destiny only if we realize we are co-creators of the universe (Pittenger 1979: 10). This intimate involvement is not on a 'head' level, we feel our way into the process of becoming and both the world and ourselves are involved in this process. Nothing is static as we stand in empathetic relation to our past, and create our future.

Whitehead's point is that though we are distinctive we are not separate from the rest of the cosmos. Therefore, anything that deepens our understanding and self awareness also contributes to our understanding of the world and vice versa. The more we understand, the more we will know we are connected to all things. This is a far cry from Greek philosophy or Cartesian thought where knowledge gained by using the head separates us from everything else, even the physical side of our natures.

Within Whitehead's world, static views are ruled out as mistaken. If we are part of the evolutionary process of the cosmos then by definition we cannot be still, nor can our understanding of things be frozen in time. For Whitehead, searching for absolutes is the central mistake since the reality of things *is* the process (1929: 11).

If we accept Whitehead's view, then two points become fundamentally important. First, things may be fresh, varied and rich in meaning, yet still carry within them some degree of continuity. Whitehead liked to refer to genuine continuity in the midst of flux, which is not unlike the Hindu realization of the dance of Shiva or the atomic physicists' realization that atoms dance and change yet preserve continuity and integrity. Secondly, decision making is of crucial importance in shaping the future. Decisions have consequences and nothing can remain the same once decisions have been made.

Process Thought is certain that everything combines to make a unity of some sort and that this unity is more inclined towards order than anarchy. Therefore, it looks for the patterns in things rather than exclusive conclusions. Old models of metaphysics were concerned with finding all-inclusive conclusions, seeing perfection as a static changeless absolute. This inevitably led to the establishment of absolutes, of norms, of views of right and wrong which fed the fires of discrimination, notably racism, sexism and many other 'isms', since anything other than a changeless absolute is bound to be found wanting. Process Thought starts with experience, our deeply intuited awareness of what it is like to experience human life. Generalizations are then made on the basis of what is known and change is always possible since our experience will constantly alter. This places metaphysics in a new mode, away from the head and disembodied reasoning and into human experience and empathetic feeling.

But what is it that our experience tells us? Despite the fact that we can only experience segments of knowledge we can see patterns emerging if we compare our experience with that of others. Some of the things we conclude are that

- we are intimately interrelated with others
- we fit into the natural order
- we are becoming—change is part of our being
- we seek goals
- we have and experience emotions
- we are capable of rational enquiry
- we are affected by our surroundings
- we sense intuitively that love will move us to a positive action more than force

- we are decision makers
- our decisions have consequences for which we take responsibility

It is important to realize that process thinkers do not view consensus as mere wish fulfilment but rather as being indicative of the way things really are. Therefore, we can feel that the world is an inter-relational place, moving towards its own becoming, as we are towards ours. The decisions we make influence, not only ourselves, but the cosmos as a whole. Everything matters.

Naturally such a philosophical stance will greatly influence any area into which it is integrated. This is true not only of science, education and psychology, but also of ethical theory and morality. An increasing number of Jewish and Christian theologians have used the insights provided by Process Thought to look again at the basic tenets of religious faith. Whitehead, himself, had certain views about the energy we term 'God' when seen through process eyes.

In *Process and Reality* Whitehead encourages us to view time as the moving image of eternity rather than a vehicle of perpetual perishing. God is not the 'unmoved mover' of Aquinas, static in this time reality, whom we can move towards or away from in our living and limited time. Nor is God the eminently 'Real' in this ever moving sea of time. Whitehead views the combination of those strands of thought in Christian theology as a great tragedy since it gives the impression of an unconnected Being who imposes his will upon us. That God should be 'unmoved' is an unacceptable enough notion for Process Thought, which sees everything in flux, but that God should be unconnected is worse, since our basic human experience speaks to us of connection. If we see God as both unmoved and unconnected Whitehead believes we begin to see God as the exception to all metaphysical principles and as a Being to be invoked to save the whole system from collapse. This does not seem to be consistent with our experience and can therefore be questioned. Whitehead cannot feel God to be that remote and therefore cannot place God before all creation but has to place God with all creation as the fellow companion and sufferer, who understands; God is not sitting above the world in judgment but is involved in the becoming of the world: 'He does not create the world, He saves it: or more accurately, he is the poet of the world, with tender patience leading it by his vision of truth, beauty and goodness' (Whitehead 1929: 346).

This God is not a God of judgment but one who makes all things new (Rev. 21.5). This God is a God in creative motion. According to Whitehead it has to be this way since our natures are 'fluid' and if we declare God to be 'static' we are faced with a contradiction, the contradiction that something which is fluid cannot be in relation with something that is static. Any philosophy based on such a view would be an illusion. The connection between God and the world is too real to be a mere appearance.

Whitehead believes there are three strands of thought in the formation of theistic philosophy. Put simply these are: God as the imperial ruler, God as the personification of moral energy and God as the ultimate philosophical principle. As a process thinker he is not happy with any of these and when he looks to the person of Jesus he is able to show why he is unconvinced. To Whitehead, Jesus shows a God in process, a God who is relating, in love, to a world in motion. He says:

> There is, however, in the Galilean origin of Christianity yet another suggestion, which does not fit well with any of the three main strands of thought. It does not emphasise the ruling Caesar, or the ruthless moralist, or the unmoved mover. It dwells upon the tender elements in the world, which slowly and in quietness operate in love; and it finds purpose in the present immediacy of a kingdom not of this world. Love neither rules, nor is it unmoved; also it is a little oblivious as to morals. It does not look to the future; for it finds its own reward in the immediate present (Whitehead 1929: 349).

By emphasizing love Whitehead brings in the possibility of relationship since love depends on those it loves. The Greek concept of God, the Absolute, who relies on moral righteousness is eliminated. God's moral righteousness in Process Thought is not judgmental but is about faithfully and persistently wanting the best for the loved one.

Whitehead also finds in Jesus the insight that man is active for human redemption. God is the chief causative agent but not the only one and Jesus is significant because he provides the classical example of what is already and everywhere operative. This is the organic involvement of the deity with the world and human existence as a move towards love. With this understanding process thinkers find themselves rejecting supernaturalism, that is, the idea that God is revealed by divine intrusions into the natural world by the occasional miraculous act. Rather God is everywhere and the true Christian will welcome his 'incognitos' (Pittenger 1979: 146).

In Process Thought, if one affirms the infinity of God, one is affirming the limitlessness of love, and not that God is entirely unlimited or beyond all knowing. It is this limitlessness of love that is the base of God's righteousness and therefore the crux of our ethics. Our ethical task is to develop our capacity for love and loving. This, of course, is something we can do best in relation to others. Process Thought sees the purpose of creation as developing the possibilities of loving relationships at every level. The important element is that we expand our ability to love, not that we conform to some absolute value. We can certainly learn from our moral heritage in this task but we must not be tied to it since the world we now inhabit is in flux. Every generation has new knowledge and a new way of being that may modify earlier moral convictions. What we always need to bear in mind is that we live in concrete and particular circumstances and that therefore our relations cannot be conducted at the level of moral abstraction. It is in this way that Process Thought combines the concept of justice with that of love. Love can, and often does, remain a comfortable abstraction but when it is connected with our becoming or our concern for the becoming of others it is manifest as a commitment to justice in the world. By the same token sin is no longer breaking rules laid down by an abstract Being but is a violation of love. Moral evil is disregard of others and a falsely self-centred preference for immediate gains without respect for the common good. So evil, within Process Thought, is no longer seen as some kind of distortion but rather as a refusal to move forward in love. Jesus, for Pittenger, exemplifies the opposite, since he moved ever forward in love and by so doing became the living Christ without ceasing to be the Man of Nazareth (Pittenger 1979: 109).

Process Thought and Feminist Theology

Process Thought has been criticized for bringing in the old absolutes of theism—belief in a God with or without a special revelation—under different names and for not relating directly to women. While there may be some truth in these criticisms there is still much that feminist theology can gain from it. First, as with feminism Process Thought makes experience central. How we experience our reality must dictate how we make our theology. Certainly Whitehead did not have women exclusively in mind when he put experience at the centre of his vision of reality, indeed he may have felt that male experience of the world could stand for human experience of the world. Today, however, feminism can go beyond this and point out that this is unacceptable; women's experiences need to be placed at the centre of theological reflection.

Second, the notion that the world is in process also removes the stereotypes of sin heaped on women. If the world was never perfect then a woman, Eve, could not have caused the downfall. This also ties in with placing our experience as central, and not seeing women as the great seducers and bringers of chaos into God's otherwise ordered world. The idea of growth and becoming is a reality with which most women are able to empathize.

Third, Whitehead referred to God and the world in mutual relation— God depending on the world as we depend on God. This is a theme which is prominent in feminist theology and expressed beautifully by Carter Heyward when she says:-

> In the beginning was God,
> In the beginning was the source of all that is,
> God yearning
> God moaning
> God labouring,
> God giving birth
> God rejoicing
> And God loved what she had made,
> And God said
> 'It is good'.
> And God knowing that all that is good is shared, held the earth tenderly
>   in her arms.
> God yearned for relationship.
> God longed to share the good earth,
> And humanity was born in the yearning of God, We were born to share
>   the earth (Heyward 1982: 49).

Fourth, the process idea that specialization is a false academic distinction which is not helpful in understanding life has also contributed to feminist theology. As a branch of theology, feminist theology informs itself not only from scripture and tradition but also from social theory, economic analysis, psychology and political theory. Therefore, part of its agenda is to broaden the horizons of patriarchal theologians to show that the knowledge of God is revealed in human existence.

Finally, Whitehead dared to use imagination in his theorizing and to envisage God as poet. A number of feminist theologians (for example Mary Daly, Dorothee Sölle, Sally McFague) are encouraging imagination in the creation of theology; they are likely to see the theologian as artist rather than source of objective, rational, absolute truth.

Process Thought provides a strand that enables women to claim 'our process as our process' and in so doing to experience a living and moving God once more, rather than the fossilized, absolute God of patriarchal religion.

Liberation Theology

While Process Thought reintroduced the moving and active God who is relating in love, Liberation Theology has taken up the notion of love as justice. Up until the 1960s the prevailing theological view within the RC Church was that society could not be changed by political means. Indeed, there was almost a theological resignation to social order, even if it was a grossly unfair social order. There is a ghastly hymn that speaks about God being quite happy with 'the rich man in his castle, the poor man at the gate'—both would receive their ultimate reward in heaven as circumstances on earth were seen as being of little consequence.

In contrast to the theological view of the static nature of society, there were developments in European theology. In the wake of political events, World War II, and church events such as the second Vatican Council, the so-called grace and nature debate suggested that man had the potential to transcend himself in himself and therefore had the right to living conditions which would give him freedom for this. And further, that the world mediates grace and one should therefore strive to eliminate injustice. At the Medellin Conference in 1968 in Columbia, South America, the Roman Catholic Latin American bishops openly challenged the situation of injustice and poverty in their countries. As Gustavo Gutierrez, the Peruvian priest and theologian, subsequently said, theology is attempting to answer questions about God, but the questions posed about God come from our situation today. So just how do you tell people in extreme poverty suffering extreme injustice that God loves them? How do you talk about this in an adult way which will enable them to take measures which would make a difference in their lives? Dogma, he says, does not tell them the 'Good News' in a way that makes sense of their concrete existence. We have seen that some strands in theology simply accept the injustice equation as part of God's plan. Other strands state that it is not God's intention, but that the world is so evil a place that such injustice is bound to occur. Yet another strand, Christian asceticism, simply declares the world evil and encourages us all to abandon it by aspiring to spiritual heights.

Liberation Theologian Leonardo Boff argues for a Christian revolution that challenges theologians and politicians to stop perceiving the world as evil and to start introducing measures to change it. By taking seriously the humanity of Jesus, Boff focuses on the fact that Jesus worked hard on his surroundings to bring about a change towards the Kingdom of God as a reality in the here and now. In this way Liberation Theology can be seen as 'incarnational', the reality of God-in-flesh means that history matters. Liberation Theologians argue that the Hebrew Scriptures show God working in history but with the incarnation of God in the Jesus, the man, we can be left in no doubt as to the connection between history and salvation—salvation is an event in history; or indeed many events in history. Jesus, we are told, showed us how to become 'sons of god' (yes, Liberation Theologians unfortunately do use the non-inclusive phrase!) and that implies that history and the living of our lives here and now have salvific significance.

Liberation Theologians stress both contemplation and commitment to others. Out of our contemplation of the divine we reflect on the concrete situations in which we see ourselves and other people and this leads to our making theology, which in turn has to be tested against concrete reality. Traditional theology does not begin by contemplating the concrete reality of individuals but rather by focusing on God.

Liberation Theology also accepts as a basic tenet that human nature is graced and free. Process Thought can assist here by emphasizing that everything is in the process of becoming, rather than in a state of disintegration and a fall from grace. This optimism about human nature is biblically based in that God created all things and saw they were very good (Gen. 1.31). The freedom that is also part of human nature can be used to transform dehumanizing situations. The reason we would want to use our freedom in this way is because we acknowledge that all people are grace-filled and that everybody is committed to everybody else. Within the framework of Liberation Theology, therefore, it is not possible to speak of 'pure faith' since a faith without a social commitment is seen as empty. Jesus, himself appeared to be advocating this by saying: 'Not every one who says to me 'Lord, Lord,' shall enter the kingdom of heaven, but he who does the will of my Father who is in heaven' (Mt. 7.21).

We are left in no doubt as to the meaning of this when we are encouraged to pray 'Thy kingdom come, thy will be done *on earth* as it is in heaven' (Mt. 6.10).

Contemplation leads to commitment; because faith and prayer are human activities, they need to be rooted in positive action directed at bringing the Kingdom of God to people in real life situations.

Liberation Theology is often accused of being Marxist. It certainly uses a Marxist method of analysis in that it recognizes that if people are to be in a position to realize their true potential they need to be freed from exploitative systems, which in the Latin American context means exploitative capitalism. As such the label is fair. However, the Marxist label has become a convenient weapon in the armoury of opponents of Liberation Theology, both ecclesiastical and secular, who feel the very mention of the word 'Marxist' will discredit its proponents, and to a certain extent they have been proved right. Dom Helder Camara has highlighted the ludicrous nature of such labelling by reflecting that if he speaks about the poor he is seen as a holy person but if he asks about the reasons for their poverty, he is accused of being a communist. 'If I give to the poor, I am called a saint. If I ask why he is poor, I am called a communist.' Such accusations can be countered with biblical references:

> I was hungry and you gave me food; I was thirsty and you me drink... (Mt. 25.35).

> No man has ever seen God, if we love one another, God abides in us and his love is perfected in us (1 Jn 4.12).

The exodus of the people of Israel, the historical event, is used in Liberation Theology as an example of an event that changed people's situation; they became active in creating their history. God did not leave them in captivity promising rewards after death; God took them to the land of milk and honey, using very human forces—the determination of the Israelites and the leadership of Moses. Another form of exodus experience is healing. Jesus healed people, he made their living conditions better for them. He also commissioned his followers to do the same, and indeed to do greater things than he had done—to act within the world and effect change.

God acts in the world in historical circumstances and this divine creative movement needs to be recognized. Gutierrez is at pains to point out that Liberation Theologians must not develop some kind of idealized picture of the poor as people who are noble and with no human failings. This, he says, would be quite unacceptable. Rather, we should recognize the humanness of the poor and be committed to them not because they are good, but because God is good. Further, Jesus showed in his life a commitment to justice, which was also central to his preaching, He sought to defend the rights of all but especially the poor, lowly, sick and alienated. If people accept that this was his stance then they will be filled with moral outrage when they see injustice and marginalization of others.

It is at this stage that two further points of Liberation Theology become crucial. They are universality and preference. Universality reminds us that no one is outside the love of God, even those who are creating the situations of exploitation and marginalization. Indeed, it is their salvation that is as much at stake as the salvation of the exploited. The liberation of the oppressed also liberates the oppressor. Preference is a thought process that makes us realize that the world and its problems are too big for us to deal with on our own, therefore we need to choose our primary allegiance. Universality and preference complement one another since a theology based purely on universality is far too abstract while one based on preference enables us to reflect upon our situation and to find the place in which we will strive to create love that is justice.

Liberation Theology calls the church to task by saying that, if it is true to the 'Good News' proclaimed by Jesus, it will be open to all, even the most marginalized, because Jesus was himself totally open. The church therefore cannot be a static hierarchical institution as this flies in the face of both process and liberation thought. The church model of liberation speaks of a church that grows out of the people. This is not to say that the people are the only source of the church, but rather that it 'rises and rises again from the people by the power of the Spirit' (Gibellini 1987: 31). These new communities of faith arise from the grass roots, championing the causes of the people, realizing a new way of relating as community and celebrating faith and life.

This, of course, moves the whole axis of the church from being associated with the ruling classes to identifying with the people; and by so doing makes it a church less likely to adopt conservatism and more likely to respond to pleas for liberation from abusive structures in society. Significantly, the 'power base' is moved from the top and is recognized as lying within each individual member of the community.

For Boff, the current ecclesiastical system is characterized as 'institutional fossilization', the result of a long historical process, lacking all theological justification and now no longer capable of being corrected by minor reforms (Gibellini 1987: 33). A church that proclaims liberation has to be liberated within; it has to have a structure that ensures complete communion and participation, in which the voice of the least is heard as clearly as everybody else's and where responsibility is shared. The Roman Catholic Church has responded by declaring that the constitution of the Church is hierarchical by divine institution and that hierarchical ministry is essentially bound up with the sacrament of order (1987: 45). Liberation Theologians are regularly being summoned to explain themselves and are often suspended from their duties, yet the church still declares it stands for the 'Good News'!

Liberation Theology understands itself as dialogue between scripture and tradition on the one side and the concrete daily life experiences of the people of God on the other. It encourages people to recognize that they cannot do theology as though they lived in some abstract realm or dead corner of history—they have to be involved in their world. Further, it makes them face the uncomfortable reality that injustice is not simply an act of fate; it is caused by people's actions and therefore requires people's action to redress the balance.

Liberation Theology and Feminist Theology

The methods of Liberation Theology extended into feminist theology. At this point we would like to reflect on the words of Gutierrez, who, when speaking at the Missionary Institute in London, Mill Hill, said he found it curious that when white middle-class men 'owned' theology it was simply called theology but when poor Latin Americans did theology it was named liberation and when women engaged in it it was named feminist. He wondered if we should reject such titles and simply claim our right to 'do theology'. It has to be noted, and today it is being admitted by the practitioners, that despite talk of including the marginalized, women were not paid much regard or given much priority in Latin American Liberation Theology. Nor was the picture more positive in the development of black theology, a discipline that places black experience at the centre of the creation of theology. Black women have subsequently branched out from feminist theology to develop their own theology, which they call Womanist theology and which speaks more directly from and to their own experience.

However, using the methods of Liberation Theology has allowed women to declare their preference as postulated by Liberation Theology: to work for justice in women's lives. While the use of social sciences in examining the causes of injustice have greatly helped women understand their oppression, the acceptance of concrete reality (women's experience in this case) as a legitimate tool in theology has enabled a breakthrough. Women no longer have to accept that the limitations placed upon them and the injustices in their lives are because God orders them. They can name them as man made and ask socially relevant questions in order to create theologically sound answers. This is a revolution. Whether it is insisting on the right to choose to have an abortion or not, speaking out against pornography, incest, rape, abuse, requesting ordination or demanding adequate childcare or comprehensive and efficient health screening processes, all these become matters with theological and spiritual implications, even if all remain matters that can be socially analysed. If God is in our history, then this means our history as women, our lives lived as women in the present and in the past. This leads to a re-examination of women's past to enable women to reclaim their history, to look and ask if God has been redeeming them or if the weight of man-made oppression has prevented this redemptive action. With the tools of Process Thought, Liberation Theology and our own experience we are able to face our religious heritage and call it sexist since it limits human norm to the male sex to the detriment of the female sex. Further, we can call on it to repent, because sexism can no longer be justified. It is a sin and as such it must be renounced and overcome.

The model of church espoused in Liberation Theology, namely base communities 'doing theology', has been developed by feminist theology into 'Women-Church', which Mary Hunt defines as 'a global, ecumenical movement made up of local feminist base communities of justice-seeking friends who engage in sacrament and solidarity' (Hunt 1990: 3). Women-Church developed from small groups of women meeting in their homes for worship. The aim is to plug into those parts of the Christian tradition that take women seriously and reject those parts found to be discriminatory. These groups are committed to developing a discipleship of equals in which women can gain once more the self understanding denied to them in patriarchy and where men can learn again to be 'woman-identified'. Women-Church is also a movement that allows people to name their own religious experience, to make decisions on the basis of it and to live out these decisions in a community that provides support yet holds the individual accountable for those decisions. It allows people to become truly religious agents in the world; there is a new responsibility: a new acknowledgment that our own experience counts in finding our salvation (Hunt 1991: 160-61).

Feminist theology expanded both Process Thought and Liberation Theology in its own unique application of their methods. Neither discipline has been particularly enlightened towards women; nonetheless they both provide insights and methods that have proved valuable in the development and acceptance of feminist theology in the present day. Whatever other questions feminist theology addresses, it is fair to suggest that it is asking:

- How are women able to grow?
- What is a just outcome?
- Are we moving closer to our divine destiny?
- How do we root that in concrete reality?

While these may be some of the immediate questions, the understanding is always that as we find space for ourselves for that which offers integrity and justice, even so do we change the concrete reality of others. In finding our justice, our liberation we hold it out to others— namely the oppressors and the oppressive structures. In naming our experience we pose questions, the answering of which will radically change society.

Women's Experience as a New Norm

The exodus of the Christian church/es from history cannot be halted unless Christianity is envisaged completely differently. Believers no longer wish to suffer here and now on the promise of a better life in the hereafter. Many women among them understand their faith based on this-worldly experiences and not based on other-worldly promises. For them faith means responsibility for shaping of one's own life in the trust of God, the God to be experienced in the everyday life and in Jesus, the manifestation of the historical God.

Much of what tradition calls 'theology' is supposed 'to happen from the neck up', to use rational arguments in order to organize thoughts about other-worldly, extra-creation divine power. What characterizes feminist theology is the awareness of our experiences, the inclusion of the rest of our selves in the doing of theology. The real lives and lived experiences of women and men, their diversity and gifts, their differences and struggles, commit us 'to ask theological questions and to give feminist answers' (Storkey 1985: 85).

Basing theology in experience is not in itself a new departure. Human experience has always been the starting point for theological reflection;

indeed, scripture and tradition are only 'codified collective human experiences' (Ruether 1983: 12). We forget this at our peril as it gives power and control to systems of authority. They gain this power by 'objectifying' this collective experience and thereby suggesting that it is somehow received from beyond our experience. In this way the symbols employed by the hierarchy dictate to us what we can experience in the present and how that experience will be interpreted. Ruether points out that this is a delusion because the reality is the opposite. 'If a symbol does not speak authentically to experience, it becomes dead or must be altered to provide a new meaning' (Ruether 1983: 13).

The canon of scripture and the creeds are examples of how original human experience becomes sorted out, accepted and codified. Once formulated they become instruments of control. The ordinary believer is presented with complex formulas that are supposed to speak of personal redeeming experiences. Although it has always been the case that individuals 'reflect and select', the general body of scripture and creeds has been carried forward by tradition as guidelines for people's behaviour and belief patterns. History shows that the consequences for not accepting these 'guidelines' have often been horrific—inquisition, 'holy wars', crusades, witch hunts.

Feminist theology is not unique in claiming experience as the base for theological reflection. Its uniqueness lies in claiming women's experience as the foundation of theological reflection. It shows that scripture, creeds and tradition are more correctly understood as scripture, creeds and tradition as codified by men. Therefore, feminist theology finds them in need of scrutiny if they are to be authenticated for women. Traditionalists often claim that feminist theology is introducing new methods that are theologically unacceptable; the most unacceptable among them is placing women's experience in a central position. Actually what feminist theology is doing is remembering that theological reflection was originally reflection on personal redeeming experience and not acceptance of fossilized absolutes. With this memory women are speaking out about their own experience, their own opportunities for redemption.

To accept that Western religious tradition has failed to incorporate women's experiences is to accept the search 'for positive and constructive alternatives to sexist theology' (Christ and Plaskow 1979: 5). The alternatives are found not in books or revelations, not in pronouncements or theses (although they might be found there); they are primarily found in the lived experience of women and men. 'Because women have often shaped and understood their lives according to norms or preferences for female behaviour expressed by men, there is a sense in which women have not shaped or even known their own experience' (1979: 6). Women now have to learn to see their own experiences as normative, learning to value their feelings as good and healthy and not compare them to a false consciousness measured against a 'norm' that is not accepting their experience. Thus it will be possible for women to cast off men's generic definitions of women's aspirations and women's limitations in order to define their own very individually expressed aspirations and limitations.

Women's experience is difficult to define and this is both its strength and weakness. If we operate with the concept of equality then every individual experience has its place and value. But how can we then say it is 'normative', and thereby establish a standard? Feminist theologians would argue that we have to make universal claims far more sparingly and to be more willing to see humanity in all its diversity. Experience, then, is normative when it is authentic for the individual; as self-affirming understanding, personal individual experience becomes normative for the individual. It may have very many different expressions, it might be the acceptance of the traditional understanding of women's bodily experiences, menstruation, pregnancy, lactation, menopause and illnesses connected with the female physiology or it might be the understanding of liberation in the spirit beyond these biological givens and any combination from the one to the other. The appeal to experience as a new norm does not mean that authority is atomized. It means that authority has to be based on considerations of experience of women and men and women have to redefine their experience beyond the prescriptions of male definitions. When theology takes women's experiences seriously, it becomes a liberating action, a commitment to praxis. This is an important point as women do not find much of traditional theology credible. Why should women 'believe or adhere to a theological point of view that either fosters women's second-class status or, at the very least, is content to permit that second-class status as the norm?' (Young 1990: 62).

Old norms were based on external authority, which meant calls to conform according to set religious and societal patterns. The leap of faith that feminist theology is willing to take is the opposite: it places authority firmly within the individual's own experience, it is internal authority that guides one to truly moral action. We no longer believe that the story of the Fall, with its chain reaction of chaos and degradation, can be pinned on women because women claim their own authority as normative in the interpretation of scripture.

This goes to the heart of doing theology—the understanding of acting the faith and not just verbalizing and articulating it. The stress on experience, on the concrete situation, is the way Liberation Theology has understood doing theology. But feminist theology goes further by seeing women's experience as a norm for theology. Women have appeared in traditional theology as types—virgins, temptresses—but not as real women. This experience of stereotype, of ridicule, of impurity, of unruly behaviour is now used by women 'as a norm for or judge of any theology insofar as that theology tries to limit women's abilities' (Young 1990: 66). The old dualistic thinking in patriarchal theology stereotyped women and it is precisely this, along black and white, good and bad lines, which is exposed by feminist theology 'for what is is, half a theology' (1990: 67). Women's experience now provides the material 'for making half a theology a whole theology' (1990: 67).

To use experiences of real lives as the source of theology is to take seriously the full humanity of women. Only this will overcome dualism and patriarchy and usher in the transformation of theology from an exclusive to an inclusive practice of reflection. It will not be easy for many women and men to be guided by their own insights and no longer exclusively from outside, from teaching and doctrine. And yet we should not confuse something that is impossible with something that is merely difficult.

Just how difficult it can be to be guided by personal insight is witnessed by the outrage shown by women of colour over what they consider to be a white middle-class agenda in feminist theology. The rhetoric of beginning from experience did not, in the early days, always acknowledge that experience was affected by colour, class and sexual orientation as much as by gender. Not surprisingly womanists were among the first to point out forcefully that feminist theology is white, it uses the tools of white scholarship in order to advance the cause of white culture.

> To say that many black women are suspicious of the feminist movement, then, is to speak mildly about their responses to it. Put succinctly women of the dominant culture are perceived as the enemy. Like their social, sexual and political white male partners they have as their primary goal the suppression, if not oppression, of the black race and the advancement of the dominant culture (Grant 1989: 169).

Of course, many womanists are also wary of declaring that all that springs from black culture is in the interest of black women. There is inherent sexism and homophobia, neither of which helps women to achieve the vision of wholeness to which they aspire.

The same story of white, middle-class, heterosexual elitism can be found in any of the experience based theologies. Women from Asia, Latin America, Africa, lesbian women, disabled women are all now claiming the right to define their own experience and therefore their own theological reality. This has meant that feminist theology has grown apace and now presents us with a rainbow of liberative possibility. It is only recently that class as a category of Western experience is beginning to enter the scene in a systematic way. All this opens the debate wide and points out with increasing clarity the narrowness of the patriarchal theological agenda. The criticisms of the early feminist agenda are justified and much of the most glaringly offensive behaviour and attitudes have now been confronted and changed.

However, all this raises, rather than solves, a problem. With the constant encouragement to define women's place in the world down to the last detail some argue that opportunities for political action are being missed. It is all too easy for the opponents of feminist theology to glory in the divides among feminists. Situating ourselves in our ethnicity, orientation and culture is extremely important but it has also dispelled one notion that was very useful for the movement, that of global sisterhood. Sadly, there does not seem to be anything to replace it. Even notions of solidarity over certain issues can be hindered by the 'definition agenda': 'What is important to you may be less so to me, in the days of global sisterhood I would fight for you anyway, now I have to consider where I will be situated in that fight'. These nuances are important but not if they stop the resistance to patriarchy. It certainly is timely to remind ourselves that while not all our relationships are right relations, the enemy is patriarchy. Patriarchy has always been good at 'divide and rule' and it would be a tragedy to play into its hands. Surely there are issues, such as violence towards women, over which women can all agree and unite and proceed to build structures of solidarity.

Weaving the Webs of Non-Violent Transformation

Feminism has always been a justice issue. The aspirations of women for equality in society and in churches led to confrontation with the institutional churches which continue to withhold precisely this equality. 'Justice and peace' drives by the churches overlook the demands by women to implement just employment structures in the institutional churches. Equal opportunities as laid down by the law of the land do not exist in the churches. Therefore, one way in which Christian women have networked is through imagining and creating new models of church.

Networking is a particularly important method and one that women have always engaged in by supporting each other in unofficial groups. Networking is a method of working on the same level with each other, of engaging in activities beyond hierarchical structures, of developing one's talents not in the field of competition but in solidarity with other women and men sharing the same goal. Thus, networking always was and is a method for questioning authority but also for forwarding new ideas, which in the context of feminist theology must be about equality and justice.

Through networking women promote goals by creative non-conformity. We can distinguish various patterns which might stand quite separately or might interweave. The first could be termed the political pattern, as exemplified by The Mothers of the Disappeared, demonstrating weekly in many South-American cities against police oppression, the abduction of children and the execution of dissidents. Simply meeting, being together, informing others of what is happening, supporting each other has triggered a feeling of solidarity that leads into action, publicity and eventually change.

There are many feminist theological networks; some would not be comfortable with the title feminist but nevertheless they give women the confidence and the solidarity to move ahead. The Britain and Ireland School of Feminist Theology forwards the feminist cause through the dissemination of scholarship via summer schools, an academic journal, *Feminist Theology*, and sponsorship of a visiting scholarship and the presentation of scholarly papers at the cutting edge of the discipline. The European Society of Women in Theological Research, while not claiming to be feminist, offers opportunities for feminist scholars to discuss their work and provides support for those under pressure in institutions. The Feminist Liberation Theologians Network aims to further the global conversation of colleagues through electronic communication and informal gatherings. The Ecumenical Association of Third World Theologians [EATWOT] keeps before everyone's eyes the agenda of colour,

race and ethnicity. Networking, like everything else, is an ever unfolding process.

The second pattern might be called the church model pattern.
Women-Churches are courageous communities with new attitudes to
doing theology in this and many countries. Created by women and men
who want to be fully accepted, they experiment with ritual, with language, in order to find spiritual sustenance that they cannot find in the
hierarchical church structures. Another model was the St Hilda community, which met every Sunday evening in the East End of London. It
was an ecumenical group and was the community with the highest
public profile. But there are many others which understand Jesus'
promise 'for where two or three are gathered in my name, there am I in
the midst of them' (Mt. 18.20).

The third pattern might be called the individual pattern as it simply
denotes the individual efforts by various women and men to stay in
touch, because they are serious about transforming theology. They contribute their gifts of research, of literature, of poetry, of writing letters,
of drawing, of painting, of organizing, of speaking, of reading, of
demonstrating, of praying, of being hosts, facilitators, funders and many
more. They have purged their language of sanitized vocabulary. Col-
lusion, quiescence and complicity have been replaced by critiquing,
speaking out and mobilizing.

There might, of course, be many more patterns of networking, from
the most obvious one, the setting up of groups with membership fees
and newsletters and meetings, to high profile lobbies for the furtherance
of particular points like Women and the Church [WATCH], the organization monitoring ecclesiastical appointments of women, or St Joan's
Alliance and Catholic Women's Ordination, campaigning for women
priests in the RC Church, to local bible reading groups, to small groups
like Dorcas in London, in existence for some 20 years, studying church
documents and regularly submitting their opinion to the hierarchies.
The important factor is that these groups do exist, that women and men
come together and engage in study and dialogue undeterred by the bad
press they receive—or being cold shouldered for years. Every group,
however small, plugging into formal and informal networks, becomes
part of a growing web of praxis, rooting theology in the here and now.

Personal experience as the source of one's own authority and networking as method of forwarding each other's authority are two criteria
on which many feminists and feminist theologians agree. Today we are

faced with a pull into two opposite directions: the tenets of inclusion, of equality and justice as pronounced by the nascent Christian church and present feminist theological research on the one hand and the mechanisms employed by patriarchal church and theology, distancing women from men, on the other hand. One way of breaking down old divisions is networking across old divides.

Churches—Triangles or Circles?

When women reflect on the hierarchical model of church, they remark most often that the gifts and charisms of women remain unwanted; that although they are in posts of responsibility, women have no authority, that they are placed under too much control and have too little choice; that there is no climate of trust. What model of church, then, would meet women's expectations? If one imagines the traditional model as that of a triangle or pyramid then the new model of church favoured by feminist theologians is the circle or the sphere. It would have a centre, but not a superstructure, it would have a focal point but not a dominating authoritarian pinnacle. It will not be an unstructured structure because unstructuredness puts power in the hands of the powerful; it will be a democratic structure in which everyone is in equidistance to the centre. The feminism of equality will issue into a feminism of liberation or as Rosemary Radford Ruether puts it: 'The quest for a life-affirming, women-affirming theological reflection will no longer ask the question is something Christian but is it healthy?' (1989: 80).

On the way to an ecclesiology based on mutuality and equality, the circle, we have to analyse the reasons for the present incapacity of the churches, the triangle, to accept new points of view, new demands, new angles. A great amount of scholarship will go into researching the wider context of the reality of full acceptance of women in state and society, their political integration and participation across widely varying social and political value-systems. One of the core questions in this discussion will relate to developments in society and their impact on religion, notably on the high levels of authoritarianism and the arrogance of sole legitimacy that still continue to act as barriers protecting the churches as institutions against the new interpretations and insights put forward by feminist theological scholarship. Alienation from forms of worship and dissatisfaction with leadership personnel and leadership methods has not yet led to the instability of the institutions. The harmful effects of the hierarchical model of church have yet to be exposed, while the enhancing effects of the egalitarian model remain untested. Yet, the traditional method, stonewalling and immobilizing women or critics or dissenters, no longer provides the churches with an impermeable layer of protection insulating them from the developments in society and research findings in the social sciences. Theologians who toe the party line, who are rigorous in their exegesis of holy scripture and church laws, find themselves no longer accepted as pastors and ministers. Compassionate theologians, on the other hand, who do not judge but attempt to understand and value the individual believer will be sought out by others.

It is therefore of vital importance to develop strategies that help promote the acceptance of new research findings, the feminist method and the equalitarian model of church. These strategies will include:

1. Understanding how the old distancing mechanisms employed in and by the churches are harming women.
2. Questioning assumptions on the role of women held by societies and churches.
3. Unmasking the rhetoric of impending schism.
4. Producing unbiased information on the obstacles to development set in the way of women.
5. Dismantling the sexist command structures of the churches.
6. Researching women's histories and women's contributions to historical developments so far overlooked and undervalued.
7. Acting on new insights in the creation of liturgies, rituals and in training and research.
8. Placing reflection on theology in the context of women's lives.
9. Exploding patterns of prejudice.
10. Giving voice to the voiceless.
11. Supporting the oppressed.
12. Acting as leaven to achieve a transformation of church culture.
13. Introducing new values.

Liturgy

Coming together as a group of people and worshipping a deity is an age-old expression of 'service', of an act of 'doing religion'. Religious leaders drew on this need and expression of communal will by organizing worship into sets of finely-honed and patterned rituals that facilitated the participation of the people. These rituals narrowed down in time to communal singing and praying and of course rubrics laid down for the application of sacraments.

Since a number of these sacramental rituals exclude women as active participants, the area of liturgy as participation is somewhat denuded. Women have developed the participatory notion in new ways by taking the liturgy out of the church and into the community. Thus a group of women in London has celebrated Holy Week for a number of years by making their way around the city as a Way of the Cross. They visit places in the city with particular meaning to them such as the Ministry of Defence, a prison, a hospital, the Houses of Parliament, the statue of Edith Cavell and so on. The Good Friday procession becomes a re-enactment of the stations of the cross for the ordinary women living in London. The locations vary from year to year depending on the participants and the point of concern which is to be the focus. Thus the walk through the city becomes a walk of public witness, imbuing ordinary and public places with spiritual and religious meaning.

Another way of taking liturgy out of the confines of church buildings is to re-act them in the street outside church buildings. The so-called Chrisam Mass on Maundy Thursday, usually celebrated by all the priests of the diocese in the bishop's church, is seen as a decisive act. The priests are anointed with holy oils. By re-enacting the same ceremony outside the church the exclusion of women becomes highly visible. By the mere fact of celebrating the Chrisam Mass women appropriate the ritual language and action for themselves.

A third option is that of street theatre, an understanding of the secular being sacred just as the personal is political. A ceremony of foot washing, a protest march, a silent prayer vigil touching the walls of a cathedral, all these are just a few examples of women developing the whole area of communal action, of liturgy, to show their presence in the life of the church and to show how they develop the action of the people far beyond narrow parameters and rubrics of liturgical action. The Association of Inclusive Language (AIL) runs a newsletter with information on inclusive language, public witness and action liturgy.

'Our Heritage is Our Power'[1]

A tactic used by the 'winners in history' is to deprive the losers of their heritage. This is done by suppressing their language, culture, mythology

1. Chicago 1979: 249.

and history. Men have systematically applied these tactics to women. Therefore, as women our first revolutionary task is to remember— indeed, to 're-member', to put together again the fragments of our shattered past. We must realize that the pattern we see presented to us as 'natural', as the way things should be, is really a social reality imposed by and written into history by the winners. We have been encouraged to forget and so we must remember.

Scholars like Mary Daly and Daphne Hampson, for example, claim that if we apply this remembering to biblical history we find there is no place for women. Biblical redaction, they claim, has totally erased women. In the face of such sexism, the best policy is abandonment. They declare that feminist praxis is rooted in the religious experience of contemporary women and cannot derive inspiration from the Christian past (Fiorenza 1983: xviii). The damage has been done to women in history but 'the reign of healing is within the Self. The remedy is not to turn back but to become in a healing environment, the self, and to become the healing environment' (Daly 1987: 338).

However, there are others like the biblical scholar Elizabeth Schüssler Fiorenza, who are not willing to abandon the power potential that lies in women remembering their heritage. She argues that to abandon our history, particularly our authentic history within biblical religion, is to give in to oppression, since it is oppression that deprives people of their history (Fiorenza 1983: xix). Patriarchal interpretation of history has carried with it definitions concerning women, therefore it is in the interests of feminism to analyse and critique those definitions. Christian history is the history of patriarchy, and even misogyny, and as such feminist analysis needs to be brought to bear on it, not only to show its bias but also to reclaim women's story. Fiorenza does not view the task as one of discovering new sources, but rather 'rereading the sources in a different key' (Fiorenza 1983: xx). Further, scripture is not only used as a record of the past, a past dominated and codified by men, but is used as 'inspirational' in worship groups today. Therefore, if we are to be inspired, not subjugated, we need to have our methods for using scriptures. We can no longer allow them to be used as 'the legitimization of societal and ecclesiastical patriarchy and of women's divinely ordained place in it' (Fiorenza 1983: 7).

Elizabeth Cady Stanton recognized, a hundred years ago, that the Bible was unfair to the sexes. Written by men, who claim to have spoken with God, it became not just a religious instrument, but a political tool, even weapon, which helped in the subjugation of women. In her eyes, it was crucial for the women struggling to find validation in the Bible, to eliminate offensive passages. Her method in *The Woman's Bible* of removing all the non-feminist and anti-feminist passages is not one that would be used today but her understanding of the problem is still a motivating factor for feminist biblical scholars.

One of the tasks of contemporary feminist scholarship is to extract the 'content' of the message from its patriarchal 'form'. This requires a critique of the prevailing patriarchal culture as much as it requires textual analysis. For example, it is necessary to realize that the Pauline statements that imply the subjugation of women were actually responses to very specific circumstances. Once the cultural context is understood, it becomes possible to see such statements as 'situation-variable and therefore script but not Scripture' (Fiorenza 1983: 15). This, of course, is not an easy task.

Some feminist scholars reject attempting to separate form and content. Phyllis Trible chooses to concentrate on the movement of the text rather than on extrinsic historical factors. By participating in this movement she feels it is possible to find the theological meaning (Trible 1978: 8). Therefore, she does not employ a context specific critique and by implication never addresses the political aspect of biblical interpretation. Further, she only addresses in passing the problem of patriarchal language, since for her it is not a central problem. Fiorenza finds her method inadequate since it never really faces the problem of patriarchy and tradition. She sees such a method as 'in danger of using a feminist perspective to rehabilitate the authority of the Bible, rather than to rehabilitate women's biblical history and theological heritage' (Fiorenza 1983: 21).

Women have suffered under patriarchy and because of this are asking if the texts that would perpetuate such suffering can really be 'divine absolutes'. This question is translated by feminist biblical scholars into research that shows the texts not as absolutes, but as faith responses; therefore not as archetype but as prototype. This is a major shift in scholarship: 'understanding a scripture as prototype not only has room for but requires the transformation of its own models of Christian faith and community' (Fiorenza 1983: 33). As the ones who are looking to transform scripture understanding we have to break the silence, we have to find ways of looking beyond patriarchy by hearing the silences. This involves us in, as Fiorenza says, 'an imaginative reconstruction of historical reality' (1983: 41) as it is not only the biblical text that is patriarchal in its voice and its silence, but also its many contemporary scholarly reconstructions.

Since language plays a major role in the shaping of our world and our theology, biblical scholars address the problems of language and attempt to use more inclusive translations . For example, Rom. 16.7 has always been translated to imply that Junia was a shortened version of the name Junias, a male name in Greek. Why, when Junia was quite a common woman's name? The answer is that the text refers to Junia becoming a Christian before Paul and receiving the some authority as the apostles. Patriarchy could not imagine women receiving such authority; feminist biblical scholarship can and does.

We realize that the inclusion and exclusion of texts, the redaction of texts, proceded according to patriarchal intentions and objectives. Therefore, we could be forgiven for feeling that the activity of women is lost forever, but this is where we need to look behind the text. For example, if Junia was in a leadership role what are we to make of the famous injunction for women to keep silent? Obviously, they were speaking and presumably they were often speaking as leaders. The question to ask now is: why was there a power struggle, not why does God wish women to remain silent? Another power struggle is evident when we realize that the Gospels show Mary Magdalene as the first resurrection witness, yet 1 Cor. 15.3-5 does not mention one woman among the witnesses. Why does the Gospel of Thomas refer to a power struggle between Peter and Mary, with Peter complaining about women receiving so many revelations from Christ? (Fiorenza 1983: 57). The dispute shows that Mary, like Peter, had apostolic authority in some Christian communities. Of course, redaction got the final word and the gospels that suggested equal apostolic power for Mary were removed. The remaining text reflected the winning side.

What we have to keep in mind is that patriarchal documents do not reflect historical reality 'as it really was'. They do contain 'theological interpretations, argumentations, projections, and selections rooted in a patriarchal culture' (Fiorenza 1983: 60). However, some texts are less patriarchal than others and can provide clues about women's roles. Some scholars have suggested that these texts may have had women authors. For example, Adolf Harnack argues that Priscilla and Aquila were the most likely authors of Hebrews (Fiorenza 1983: 61). This is a very important finding for women, because it allows us to imagine that apostolic authority could be vested in women. But it does not automatically overcome the patriarchal assumptions in the texts and therefore, we should not fall into the error of declaring all women authors free of their cultural influences.

Feminist biblical scholarship does not only enable us to 'find the women' in Christian beginnings but to locate the power struggles behind the texts. They were struggles that women lost but looking and finding them can be an empowering experience for contemporary women. We no longer have to be told and have to accept that God gave us a secondary position, we have to examine instead how patriarchy manipulated us into that position. Once we remember that the reality was radically different we can begin to move forward and be stronger with the knowledge we have. Fiorenza's hermeneutic of suspicion has been a huge help for women attempting to engage with their traditions. It is both scholarly and accessible and above all it makes alternative readings possible.

Women of colour have also been recovering their own history both as historical fact and as biblical narrative. The situation within a text of a woman carrying experiences other than those of the dominat culture leads to very challenging readings. For example, women of colour, who sit with the Syro-Phoenician woman, understand Jesus to be exhibiting sexism and racism, the references to dogs can be less easily spiritualized when such words of abuse are part of one's everyday life. Hagar has also been claimed as a woman who highlights the myth of global sisterhood, she is doubly abused both as a surrogate and as a scapegoat. Sarah is not her ally.

Postcolonial readings of the texts (cf. Kwok 2000) are now almost mainstream and, of course, they add yet more grist to the mill. In the wake of de-colonization in the 1960s a process set in that began the de-colonization of the historical and biblical stories. Other voices are being heard and the texts are read across the grain in a fascinating and liberative way. Feminist theology has brought us a long way. We have come to realize that history is not a monosyllabic tale, it has many layers of oppression and priviledge within it. The future is a very bright one as we engage with the consequences of these varied readings and reclaimings.

Conclusion

The methods of feminist theology aim to make traditional theology liberating for women by releasing it from patriarchal assumptions. Every society and every system only grows by challenges to it. It is a legitimate task to query the situation, the status quo and even more so the sanitized picture of the status quo. One of the tasks of feminist theology is to overcome old dichotomies and to usher in an understanding of pluralism that give speech to the speechless, that empowers the powerless and lets outsiders participate.

Change there has to be. There is always change, everything is permanently in flux and dislocations are possibilities for change. If we do not learn to deal with change then how do we cope with disaster? Through struggle we discover our rights. The goal is to dismantle the prejudice of patriarchal prescriptions and with it patriarchal power. There is growing resentment against this power because of the harm being done to women in the name of religions. With the help of biblical and church historical feminist scholarship causes for sexism in the churches have been laid bare. With this conceptual tool we can proceed to look at the mechanisms that made use of one-sided views and its outcome, the customs and prescriptions based on these views.

Feminist theology as we have seen is involved in a twofold task: it is critiquing patriarchal theology and it is complementing traditional theology so as to safeguard the understanding of everybody as equal and equally suited to take his or her life experience as starting point from which to start interpreting theology. It supplies the tools to make the shift from seeing religion as controlling life to seeing it as a way of understanding life. Feminism is not about making the world woman-centred, but about bringing the world into balance, offering a way out of age-old dualisms and discrimination to achieve inclusion and mutuality.

We have to learn and unlearn certain facts, for example a dogma is not a constant belief, it is an interpretation frozen into the context of its time, it is not an 'eternal' truth, merely an interpretation placed in history. Truth cannot be gained by guilt, by denying reality, by accepting fantasy as reality. When the poet Friedrich von Schiller said 'Only error is life and knowledge is death' he expressed the truth that we have to search for truth all the time afresh and test out findings. The philosopher Karl Popper went further by calling every 'truth' simply the hypothesis to be tested and found wanting by the next generation of scientists and scholars. Many truths are held together by their own rust and crumble when touched. Many truths will have to be rewritten in a new language. This is the key agenda of feminist theology. We must take the knowledge we have as women and build on it. The Liberation Theologian Gustavo Gutierrez encourages us to drink from our own well. If we start with the tradition of discrimination and hold it up against an understanding of ourselves and our lives, we have to ask: 'Which is more plausible?'

The constant questioning of received truth and wisdom is a project that is not that of feminism alone. Postmodernism has just such a task as its life blood. Indeed, many feminist theologians are using the methods of postmodernism in their work and often criticizing the older generation of feminist theologians for not embracing it with joy. Everything is open to question and every institution open for criticism, a positive step perhaps. Each truth claim carries as much weight as the next and it is only the ability to argue that makes one win out over the other. It would be foolish for feminist theology to attempt to overlook the postmodern discourse, it is all around us. However, it may be equally foolish to embrace it wholeheartedly. Beverley Harrison is cautious; she is concerned that the political edge is lost when we are required to accept all truth claims as equal. For her feminism is more than one truth claim among others: it is a political agenda set against the worst excesses of the patriarchal mindset and actions. She does not wish to accept as valid fundamentalist claims that reduce the self esteem and agency of women or at worst mutilate their bodies. Instead she would like to campaign for the elimination of such ways of life (Harrison 1999). The meeting of postmodernism and feminism brings into sharp relief the age-old question that has always been part of the debate: if we begin with experience where do we draw the moral line? It is evident that patriarchy suits a great number of men and women; do we as feminist have to respect that and let it rest? The dilemma is highlighted in a joke going around the academic world. 'I am being tortured', says the victim of oppression. 'That's interesting', says the postmodern scholar! Where is the passion that has been the life blood of social change? Feminist theologies found life from passion and it will be a sad day if they become coldly objective in their engagement with truth claims and the worlds that they bring about.

Chapter 5

What's in a Word?

Language, like many other things with which we are familiar, can be taken for granted. We may begin to assume that we know what is meant and so we no longer look closely at what is conveyed by the words we use.

In an introduction to feminist theology it is important to examine language from two angles. First, to explore how the language used about God has shaped the concept of deity and influenced the position of women, and second to see how women are now using 'God-language' in an effort to reshape the concept of God and the world.

Psychologists ceaselessly debate the nature of language and the effect it has on our thinking. Although their theories differ they all agree that language and thought are intimately bound together. It is beyond our present purpose to examine minutely psychological arguments in order to find one theory that stands the test of enquiry. It is sufficient to acknowledge that the debate hinges on whether language determines the concepts we develop or whether it simply reflects cultural concepts.

Sapir and Wharf believe that things that are fundamentally important in cultures are given great attention in language. For example, snow plays a central role in Eskimo life and so there are 27 words to describe it ranging from drifting snow to fluffy snow to packed snow. A further example of how life and language are linked can be found in the Zulu language. It contains no words for square or rectangle and research has found that the concepts are also absent in the culture. This is because the Zulu world is round; round huts; round windows and doors and round village lay-outs. Researchers found that in relation to this Zulus perceive angles very differently from those of us who live in the Western world. In the light of this it may be interesting to reflect that the English language has over 200 words for women who own their sexuality and express it as they wish (standard English calls such women promiscuous) while only 20 words exist which describe men who act in the same way (Hartland 1991: 38). Surely this is not simply an accident! When we realize that the words used for women are not ones that conjure up positive images, while some of the male terms do, we are further led to believe that the language is loaded with a strong message.

If language does draw attention to features in our environment that are important we can easily be forgiven for assuming men are important, while women are less so. The most simple example of this is the use of 'man'as a generic term for both sexes. Spender (1982b) strongly argues that language makes women invisible and in so doing devalues the person but also the attributes of that sex, for example nurture and inter-connection when thinking of women. Those who would argue that we all realize 'man' is a generic term have been proved wrong by research (Martyna 1986) which shows that using 'man' or 'he' influences people to conjure up masculine images. When shown pictures of men and women that were accompanied by general statements about the human race using 'man', all those tested thought the statements applied only to the men.

When we realize how many crucial concepts use the generic term and therefore exclude women the problem becomes more serious. It is not about 'manhole' or 'personhole' as the tabloids would like to suggest. It is more fundamentally about 'manpower; craftsman; the thinking man; man in his wisdom; statesman; masterful; the brotherhood of man; sons of free men; Liberty, Equality, Fraternity; faith of our fathers; God the Father and Son of God'. The list is endless. The point is that in language when applied to things of importance women are invisible and if the research is correct women are invisible because we are not believed to be concerned or connected with things of importance.

Gloria Steinem does point to certain changes in language brought about by feminism, for example, centre, newspaper, network or rock band may now have 'women' placed in front of them and be taken seriously, whereas 15 years ago such phrases were put-downs (Steinem 1984). Terms like 'sexual harassment' and 'battered women' have been introduced when beforehand these conditions were just known as 'life' (1984: 149). 'Lesbian-mother' was seen as a contradiction in terms. She also points out that judgmental words such as frigid or nymphomaniac have been replaced with non-judgmental words like pre-orgasmic and sexually active (1984: 153). However she is in no doubt that there still is a long way to go with language. Words, loaded with meaning, have the power to exclude.

Words and naming also have the power to imply ownership. Marriage ceremonies, although more flexible than they were, still suggest ownership. The title Mrs gives a clear idea of whose property one is. Indeed, even if women do not accept the husband's name at marriage their own name is still that of a male relative, their father's. Throughout European history, the process of name giving was a process of claiming ownership. This is also reflected in Christianity. In baptism a child is claimed for Christ. In confirmation, the young adult is claimed for active apostleship and is given a new name. In marriage, the women renounces her father's name and accepts her husband's name as a way of showing where her new duties lie. Only recently, civil law has allowed women not to change their name. This signals the realization that people entering into contracts are able to do so as autonomous individuals. The naming of slaves by slave owners is another example of how naming implies claiming. We see this also with land where 'explorers' renamed land for 'King and Country' or for their own purposes regardless of its original title.

Language also reflects perceived power. Lakoff (1975) has shown that women are encouraged to use less assertive language while boys are encouraged not to be tentative. Boys learn to be direct and decisive in their speech while girls are expected to beat around the bush especially when they speak to men. Experiments with very young girls show that children's thinking about gender appropriate behaviour is influenced by the language they hear (Ervin-Tripp and Mitchell-Kernan 1977). Spender shows that girls are less assertive in schools, thus being ignored. Boys demand attention verbally, and so in this way assertive language gains access to education (1982b: 66).

Just how our language carries assumptions can be illustrated in this well known passage:

> A man and his son were apprehended in a robbery. The father was shot during the struggle and the boy was taken in handcuffs to the police station. As the police took the boy into the station, the Chief of Police, who had been called to the scene, looked up and said 'My God, it is my son!'

When asked what was the relationship between the Chief of Police and the boy most people replied, 'father'. When reminded the father had been shot, they say illogically 'step-father'. 'Mother' is not a word that springs readily to most minds. Although Steinem asserts that now we are becoming the men we wanted to marry (1984: 149) because we are now training as doctors, engineers and deep-sea divers and we are not simply being trained to marry them, we still have a long way to go before company directors, doctors and police chiefs are thought of as women.

A more disturbing trend can be observed by asking groups of people to make two lists, one containing words containing female qualities the other male qualities. That such lists can be written at all is depressing but that they contain stereotyped images is worse. A female list would typically contain, emotional, attractive, caring, nurturing, faithful. While a male list would contain, logical, rational, assertive, strong. The most crushing blow comes when the groups are asked to write a third list under the heading Mature Adult. The lists of both men and women bear a striking resemblance to those under the heading Male Qualities. What needs to be asked is why we as women often write these lists ourselves. There are, no doubt, countless answers to such a question, but feminist theology concentrates on the theological and religious aspects while informing itself from the social sciences. A feminist theology answer might suggest that Western culture has been influenced by Christianity and its gender related views of God, which has projected a stereotyped view of human nature. Such an answer obviously needs explanation.

Naming the Nameless

The power of language is immediately evident when we look at the Judaeo-Christian Scriptures. It is through speaking and naming that God created the world (Gen. 1). The idea is developed in the Christian scriptures with 'the Word' being in the beginning and actually being God (Jn 1.1). Words have the power to create human reality; to shape our world. In certain cultures naming a child is a matter of deep spiritual significance; since the name we receive is believed to shape our character and fate.

The power of naming has been acknowledged as crucial by feminists since it not only expresses and shapes our experience but also gives us the power to transform our reality. We believe we are completing the partial picture as so far the naming has been done by men and so remained inadequate since they can only name their reality that we know is not always ours. Literature that is written by men and in the service of male monotheism must reflect the language and the concepts of patriarchy. The Hebrew Scriptures confirm the fact that men have named reality (Gen. 2.19-20) by showing Adam indulging in just that activity; he even names Woman (Gen. 2.23). Within Judaeo-Christian history the power of naming prevails! 'The sacrament of baptism has its roots in the practice of ritual bathing in Jewish synagogues and homes' (Buckley 1978: 12). While the ritual bathing remains, another element, that of name giving has become central. The physical act of birthing, which is held to be material and female, and therefore the opposite of spiritual and male, has to be remedied and this can only be done by a man, the priest, who pronounces the removal of original sin: through the power of naming a new birth is proclaimed that is considered superior to the physical birth.

As with any piece of literature it is important to place the Hebrew Scriptures in context. Traditionally the context is that nothing existed and God created; and what was written down by a faithful scribe came directly from the mouth of God. Biblical scholarship and archaeological evidence point beyond this type of fundamentalist argument. We have to ask 'What was the context?'

Archaeological evidence suggests that the most ancient human image for the divine, found throughout the Mediterranean world, Western Europe and India, was female. The statuettes and images featuring enlarged breasts, buttocks and abdomens are commonly interpreted as pictorial and sculpted representations of Goddesses. We are simply in the dark whether the images were used for cultic purposes or dynastic ones. But it is fairly safe to assume that representations of Goddess were not necessarily personified, but rather symbolic of the mysterious power of life. The enlarged abdomens, the source of being, the great womb in which all things come to be, ensure that this divine image is not abstracted to a world beyond but is 'the encompassing source of new life that surrounds the present world and assures its continuance' (Ruether 1983: 48).

Excavations have unearthed statuettes and images of female deities dating from the time of 6500 to 3000 BCE. The cult of the Goddesses in cultures like Sumer and Babylonia became paired with a male deity. The images of the divine came to reflect the social order of ruling classes which emerged with increasing urbanization. Both God and Goddess are seen as images of sovereign power to which the worshipper relates as a subject petitioning for favours (Ruether 1983: 49). Despite this shift in relation between divinity and humanity the relation between God and

Goddess remains the same; there is no notion of complementarity or equality. Gender division is not part of the divine realm—both Gods and Goddesses have power as well as the ability to nurture. Although creation myths declared the defeat of the Goddess, such as the Marduk-Tiamat story, they were always balanced by others so that the Goddess was still seen as a positive force representing not only fertility but wisdom and the bringing together of the human and divine order. It is this positive image and the world view it creates that stands in stark contrast to that portrayed by male monotheism.

If we understand this background we can look at the Genesis story with new eyes and see the power struggle that it reflects. It is believed that male monotheism has its roots in an understanding of God as a Sky-Father of nomadic tribes, warrior clans, moving with their herds and defending them but lacking the understanding and valuing of gardening, replenishing the soil, storing surplus, all the activities of agricultural societies, in which women were the stewards of the land (Ruether: 1983: 53). Whatever the origins we see the Goddess being subdued in Genesis. A male God hovers over the waters, which is a female principle, and created, as if from nothing. The Goddess is nameless, she has no role in the process of generation. By not naming, the role of the female in the origins of the world is lost. The story relies on the intercession of a serpent, which is viewed as deviant. However, in Goddess imagery the serpent is wise and symbolizes regeneration because of its ability to shed its skin. As a symbol for the Goddess it also signifies healing, and still today the medical profession has as a symbol the caduceus, which is a staff with a snake entwined around it. Within the context of Goddess worshipping cultures it would have been quite understandable and acceptable that the serpent should encourage the woman to seek knowledge. There would be nothing evil in the notion that having sought it, divine attributes would be received. However, the biblical story is written from the point of view of male monotheism and so the consequences of these 'Goddess pursuits' are disastrous; the whole order of things is thrown into turmoil and the human race is punished. The serpent, the wise noble representative of the Goddess, is thrown on its belly in the dust (Gen. 3.14) and woman, the representative of the Goddess, is punished. What was the greatest symbol of the divine power of the Goddess, birth, is to become a source of agony for woman (Gen. 3.16) and her equal partnership with man is to be dissolved, she is to be controlled (Gen. 3.17). Further, what was a source of joy and a symbol of divine power to humans—their physical bodies—are now sources of shame (Gen. 3.7; 21) The patriarchal God is 'above and beyond', he strongly influences humans to move away from the physical plane by encouraging them to step away from their physical natures in shame.

Leadership qualities, in the context of the Jewish reality male warrior leadership qualities, were projected onto the highest leader, the tribal God of Israel. The Genesis story does not merely relegate women to a secondary position, it also attaches negative connotations to female nature: it is material. The material worldly aspect of the Goddess, which was viewed as being the origin of divine power, birthing, was punished with pain. The Goddess, and with her women, has been subdued.

Symbols which were used in Goddess worship were not entirely eradicated, although their functions were altered. For example, the sacred marriage between the God and Goddess is used to symbolize the relationship between God and the people. While the format remains, the essence of its meaning is drastically changed from one of creative, powerful equality to one where the female partner is reduced to human level and the male partner is depicted as judgmental and angry towards his harlot wife (Ruether 1983: 55). This illustrates quite well the power of patriarchy; it reduces creative equality to blame-filled dominance.

This notion of dominance and 'power-over' is developed throughout scripture. Titles like king are used, which imply a truly unequal power base. A king rules his subjects with absolute power and authority. There is no power sharing, he is removed from his people and dictates their futures while being minimally affected by their lives. There is the added consequence that kings can use military power to secure their own ends; in the same way God the King can and does use such tactics. He uses them throughout the pages of the Hebrew Scriptures and his male representatives have spoken of, and declared, 'just wars' ever since. The king image holds problems for feminist theology as we can see.

Even where Goddess images remain, they no longer depict autonomous, female manifestations of the divine, but rather secondary qualities of male deity. This can be illustrated in the book of Proverbs where Wisdom, which was originally the characterization of the Goddess, is taken to be the offspring of God. She is the vehicle through which the transcendent God is mediated. Therefore she keeps her connection between the human and divine, but in patriarchy this diminishes her rather than exalts her. When Wisdom (Sophia) is referred to in Christian scripture, she is removed yet another step from her Goddess roots.

Sophia is replaced with the masculine word logos, so although the attributes remain the same—revealer of God to humanity—she is masculinized. Since this title is also attached to the male person of Jesus, we now see a man standing where Wisdom once stood as the revealer of God; this time both the revealer and the revealed revelation are male. This is a long way from Goddess who in the serpent imagery is Wisdom.

Language shapes reality and the structure we see emerging under patriarchy is one of hierarchy and dominance. This does not simply describe the relationship between the sexes but describes the entire social order. The male transcendent God looks down upon a hierarchy in which masters rule slaves; kings rule subjects; certain races colonize others; men rule the earth and humanity exploits all living creatures. Patriarchy is 'us' and 'them'—'us' rule in the name of God and 'them' can submit or be damned. Dualism is set firmly in place and so the patriarchal God has literally split the cosmos in two, between spirit and matter. All that is lesser is connected with feeling and sensing and matter and all that is valued is spirit and by definition of a higher order and removed from matter, the pinnacle of God. By gendering God as exclusively male the whole social order is in turmoil. Although God is seen to be on the side of the oppressed, they are 'his people'. The prophets often speak against classism (Mic. 4.4), but never against sexism. Many use symbolism that once was Goddess symbolism in a very sexist way.

The prophet Hosea uses the symbol of the sacred marriage by comparing his own marriage to an unfaithful woman with Yhwh's marriage to Israel (Hos. 1.2). Hosea is faithful, loving and forgiving, as is Yhwh, but the wife continues to run after other lovers, as Israel continues to lust after other Gods. Both Hosea's wife and Israel have become whores, but because Hosea tries to show his faithfulness, he buys her back (3.2). The implications of this story are that woman is a possession; if she tries to express her autonomy, the consequences are disastrous—she becomes a whore; by buying her back he treats her like chattel; he reclaims her not through love, but through a transaction, in which she has no stake. Although the image of sacred marriage is being used, the implication is ownership by God, the male of Israel, the female. This is a long way removed from the original understanding of equality where Goddesses and Gods shared in creation.

The language of the Hebrew Scriptures gives a definite picture and shapes a certain reality—God is male and appears to be the colour of the dominating race, which under biblical guidance has tended to be white. This interpretation can develop into harsh views of supremacy, for example in South Africa where the Dutch Reform Church quoted scriptures to justify apartheid and in the US where the Ku Klux Klan quotes biblical texts that advocate separation and white superiority. The Klan is quite clear regarding the position of women; there is no question of equality, the white male is as close to God as it is humanly possible to get.

Jesus showed signs of regaining the mutual relating that was evident in Goddess religion by calling God Abba or 'Daddy'. In this way he signalled that God was not the remote judgmental figure grown of the Hebrew Scriptures. Rather, he is affectionate with his children, he nurtures them but still receives respect. The language softens the vengefulness of a king and warrior and allows followers to be children, not cowering subjects. Jesus also says 'No longer do I call you servants... but I have called you friends' (Jn 15.15) which once again reverses the prevailing patriarchal view. Divinity is not pictured as sovereignty but as friendship and in terms of a loving family relationship. This view has social implications. No man is to be called father, master or lord (Mt. 23.1-10) since everyone is part of the 'friendship group'. Further, family relationships, which were set up to serve patriarchy, are no longer binding. People are called to leave such a system in order to relate more fully to a new community of brothers and sisters (Mk 3.31-35). From the language used we are given a vision, one that is based on equals who lovingly interact between themselves and with their God.

Not only is the community envisaged through language but Jesus actually includes women in his teaching. A powerful example is Lk. 10.38-42 where he actually defends Mary's right to study in the circle of disciples. Ruether points out that a number of parables of Jesus include women and highlight the equality of male and female. The Parable of the Lost Coin (Lk. 15.8-10) does not image the woman in a stereotypical way; her money seems to be her own and she is not dependent on a man. Also the image it gives of God is not patriarchal but rather as a seeker, nurturer and transformer (Ruether 1983: 68).

It would be rather extravagant to suggest that Jesus is totally imaging the Goddess in his life teaching but it is possible to say that a picture does come through of a more mutual and loving figure of God than we have grown used to in the Hebrew Scriptures. Of course, once the Jesus community became accepted into the dominant culture, which was one based on the absolute rule of Caesar, the old images re-emerged. God became king and lord and the patriarchal relationships to which such language pointed were used to justify the imposition of patriarchal domination in many areas of life. Caesar's lawyers got hold of the message of love and equality and turned it into fear and domination. As Ruether points out, Abba was lost and replaced by a series of 'holy fathers' proclaiming the kingship of God and basking in the power that title gave them (1983: 66). All the old images were reinforced and the spiritual purpose served a political one.

'Sticks and Stones may Break my Bones but Names will Never Hurt Me'

Alas, this phrase is wrong. The patriarchal God that is held up to women, hurts women not only as an image—God is male, we are not— but also because of the pronouncements that are products of the imaging. The Pauline literature and Pastoral epistles give voice to overt sexism while the Gospels are largely sexist by omission. It is made quite plain that women are to be submissive to their husbands (Tit. 2.5; 1 Cor. 11.3) and must never have any authority over a man (1 Tim. 2.12); woman is to keep silent (1 Cor. 14.34). This is because Eve was deceived and so women are unworthy transgressors. There is hope for us though 'woman will be saved through bearing children' (1 Tim. 2.15). We are evil and now we have the first sign of biology being destiny; indeed one's ultimate destiny as a woman is seen here to be dictated by biology, heaven or hell depending on the fruition of one's womb. If the author had thought it through he might have legislated for women being allowed to divorce sterile men; after all there was a lot at stake! These statements show just how as women our bodies have been attacked by patriarchy. Woman is linked with matter, echoes of the Goddess, but as we have seen within patriarchy this is inferior, in need of control. The patriarchal interpretation of God shines through when we read 'slaves to be submissive to their masters' (Tit. 2.9). This is in direct contradiction of Jesus, who declares that in the new community you call no one master. The message implies the patriarchal hierarchy quite explicitly 'Remind them to be submissive to rulers and authorities' (Tit. 3.1) which is very disappointing for those who understood Paul's declaration in Galatians that 'there is neither Jew nor Greek, there is neither slave nor free, there is neither male nor female; for you are all one in Christ Jesus' (3.28) to be one of equality. As we have seen, this may not have been the true meaning. Christian tradition has chosen to ignore any hint of radical equality that may have been present in the early tradition and has concentrated instead on patriarchal hierarchy; it has suited its purpose to do so.

Feminists have attempted to deal with this innate scriptural sexism in a number of ways. The most famous pioneering effort being by Elizabeth Cady Stanton who removed all the anti-feminist passages from the Bible and published it again in 1898 as *The Woman's Bible*. More recent approaches have attempted to remove the patriarchal bias of the material by looking below and beyond the text for true meaning and the contribution of women. This kind of approach has been employed by Elizabeth Schüssler Fiorenza and Phyllis Trible (Fiorenza 1983; Trible 1984).

Not only feminist biblical scholars, also church historians have looked at misogynistic texts from the Church Fathers right through to church leaders today and published their research (Pagels 1979; Moltmann-Wendell 1986). The texts, which make up the body of 'tradition' that the churches so fervently defend, make grim reading. The language they use about women is often demeaning and abusive, one does not feel like a sister in Christ when on the receiving end of it.

The *Malleus Maleficarum*, the Witches' Hammer, notes that, as women were formed from a bent rib, they are full of deception because they are imperfect animals. The same book declares that all witchcraft springs from carnal lust which is insatiable in women. On the strength of this many thousands of women died during the Witch Craze, or burning times, from the fifth to seventeenth century in Europe.

Jerome holds out hope for women: if they serve Christ they will cease to be women and will become men! 'She who does not believe is a woman…whereas she who believes progresses to perfect manhood' (*Exposition of the Gospel of St Luke* 10.161). Ambrose echoes the idea that full humanity for women means shedding our female nature and becoming male (*Regula Episcopi*, Preface) Our sex is our sin and the expression of our sexuality leads to damnation. Martin Luther felt we could put it to good use reflecting the biblical attitude, he expressed the opinion that we should bear children until we die of it, but on no account should we enjoy their conception.

The verbal abuse of women, stereotypes of saint or harlot, negative and loaded language fed into structures that have developed as a result of language. Karen Armstrong (1986) deals fairly comprehensively with the way the structures have, historically, turned women into masochists. If the language used about women creates only negative or one-sided pictures, then structures feel justified in subduing and controlling women. They have done this physically. They have taught us to turn against our bodies and have rewarded us with sainthood according to the amount of suffering and self mutilation we are willing to undergo (Armstrong 1986: 138-39). It is frightening to realize just how willing to accept suffering many of these women have been. The power of language and resultant images has great sway over the psyche.

Susan Brocks Thistlethwaite demonstrates that this kind of masochism is still prevalent amongst biblical fundamentalists today. Due to the injunctions to be submissive to your husband these women are reluctant to remove themselves from abusive situations. A survey carried out in 1981 showed that 1 in 27 women had been raped; 1 in 13 physically abused and 1 in 4 verbally or emotionally abused (Christ and Plaskow 1989: 302). It is for this reason that Thistlethwaite believes a feminist critique of the bible is necessary; these women need to find positive images in order to gain the strength to remove themselves.

It is not only sticks and stones that hurt but words as well. Words create; patriarchal words about a patriarchal God have created our Western culture. We have seen how this has specifically affected women, but patriarchy affects everyone. All kinds of dualism are set in place that diminish people different from the dominant group or elements in life. Feminist theology wants to overcome the false divisions between spirit/matter; male/female; black/white; human/animal; humanity/nature; heterosexual/homosexual; young/old; rich/poor. It is looking for language that re-images God in such a way as to reflect the mutual and interconnected nature of reality. Ruether points out

> If God/dess is not the creator and validator of the existing hierarchal social order, but rather the one who liberates us from it, who opens up a new community of equals, then language about God/dess drawn from kingship and hierarchal power must lose its privileged place (1986: 69).

Our task, therefore, is to find language that reflects the radical interconnectedness of all creation. The language of dualism is a language laden with value judgments and as such bolsters hierarchy and the divisions between people that such a system implies. Divisions are not constructive; the goal must be to envisage a world where hierarchal division is outmoded. Along with Martin Luther King we look forward to the

day when racism, segregation and prejudice are no longer in the dictionary. As women we would add rape, incest, sexual harassment, global
warming, ecological spoliation and many more. We are a long way from
this, as witnessed by the inclusion in the Collins *Dictionary* to include
'ball-breaker' in their 1992 edition. Its inclusion is depressing, the definition is shattering: 'A woman whose *character* and *behaviour* may be
regarded as threatening a man's sense of *power*? (the italics are ours). We
live under patriarchy, even the English dictionary tells us so!

Language is important in feminist theology because it clearly shows us
how we are perceived, which is for many of us the first step to anger. It
also enables us to 'hear each other to speech'. It enables us to break our
silence. The strength women find in networks is found precisely because
they can break many silences within themselves by speaking with others.
We must do this or our empowerment will be lost. We have seen how
our history has been shaped by the words of others and now we must
begin to shape *our* history with *our* words. By gathering in groups we
begin to shape our truth and find words for feelings that have been long
buried under patriarchy.

Just how powerful language is has been demonstrated with the publication of the prayer book *Women Included*. This book shows how one
group of feminists, men and women, have struggled with language to
make it inclusive in worship. They have done this together at the St
Hilda Community in London, which is a group that uses feminist liturgy
to celebrate life. The book is not intended to cause a revolution but
before publication it was spoken about in Parliament. The Tory MP
Michael Alison declared it unlawful to change the gender of God without Parliamentary consent! There must be a lot at stake if it concerns
government.

If we are really in the process of becoming, as Whitehead suggested,
then we need language that reflects that, not that the static language of
absolute that is usually associated with religion and theology. As women
we need language that reflects our process of becoming. What we say
must make sense in terms of our life experience. It would be a grave
mistake, however, to project those terms that reflect women's experience into absolutes. Replacing patriarchy with matriarchy is not the aim
of feminist theology. Certainly some language will be useful to men in
their process and so we offer it as our spiritual gift, but we must remember that in process thought no absolutes are necessary.

What Language Shall we Speak?

Among feminist theologians Mary Daly stands out as having been most creative with language. She reclaims words from patriarchy and invents words when she feels the experience is beyond patriarchal language. She says that as a gynocentric writer she wants to give rise to intuitive play in our own space, which enables thinking that is vigorous, informed, multi-dimensional, independent, creative and tough (1987: 23). Daly plays with words and invites us to hear them again in a new way; a way that throws light on our experience as women. She takes words that have traditionally conveyed negative images of women and transforms them. 'Spinsters' are no longer unmarried women with the images that conveys, but women spinning webs of wonder and unfolding the future. Hags, crones, witches are all 'wanderlusting women' who wander through patriarchy wielding labrysses 'double axes of our own wild wisdom and wit, which cut through the mazes of man-made mystification, breaking the mindbindings of master-minded doublethink' (1984: 14). 'Dyke', she explains, is a barrier that prevents the passage of something undesirable and so Dykes stand against the passage of patriarchy. Daly takes the sting out of language that has been designed to control women and she replaces it with the desire to spark and spin.

Feminist theology needs to adopt a similiar approach to theological language making it truly liberative for women. We should look at the way language is used and dare to remove words from the realms of negativity to those of imaginative creativity. Our language must name our experience and not mold it. Women must speak out so that our reality can be heard and placed in the language of society.

Not everyone will feel comfortable with Daly's approach. Indeed, some would argue that it is a project doomed to failure since some general understanding between people is necessary if change is to occur. Developing new language in the way that Daly advocates in her *Wickedary* (Daly and Caputi 1988) could become a counter-productive exercise. Playing with words and reclaiming their positive meanings, or inventing positive meanings, is very important, while one step beyond that to invention of words may just be one step too far.

It also has to be acknowledged that there are those who believe their tradition has enough within it for meanings to be recovered from the words and concepts already there. The Judaeo-Christian tradition has many images that have been overlooked in favour of patriarchal power-filled notions. We have images of God as mother, Jesus as a mother hen and both able to midwife the believer. Both God and Jesus feel the agony of childbirth and wish to exhibit the care characteristic of a mother for her child. It was as early as the second century CE that God was envisaged as lactating and believers imagined themselves being suckled by this maternal God (Wootton 2000: 12). There is, of course, the figure of Sophia, or divine wisdom, who scholars present as the image of the female divine, which is present throughout the Hebrew Scriptures. All these are positive images of the divine and women, if rather essentialist in character. There is always the danger that in resurrecting such images we simply reinforce ideas of female motherhood and care giver as the only roles appropriate for women.

Despite this note of caution it is refreshing to hear these images in the work of modern day hymn writers such as Brian Wren (1989) and June Boyce-Tillman (with Wootton 1993). Along with the resurrection of the female divine images there has been a resurgence of biblical women, re-membered and seen as positive role models. It is surprising what an effect it can have on a congregation to hear of Ruth and Naomi, Deborah and Miriam without them being overshadowed by male figures. This naming and celebrating often helps women to name and celebrate their own experience and in so doing to gain self respect and recover self esteem. In this respect the re-membering does not always have to be positive; hearing the stories of those women gravely abused in Scripture can also have a truly transforming affect on women. Not only do they feel that their own experience is being named publically but they often gain the anger to recover and to move on in a positive way.

Feminist theology acknowledging as it does the place of experience also values the body much more than patriarchal theology has been able to under the weight of dualistic metaphysics. The body then is also considered to have a language and one that can be used in worship and in pursuit of the divine. This valuing ranges from circle dancing, the very shape of which gives a new feel to the idea of worshipping community, to the celebration of bodily matters once made taboo, for example menstruation and sex beyond heterosexual practices. Although the body has always been part of the language of worship it has undergone many reductions and restrictions. It is now being given far more freedom of expression with theologies that are more materialistic and liberative. Feminists are multi-lingual, speaking in words, body, art and music but still we are only a whisper amidst the patriarchal roar. We must keep finding new languages with which to speak and challenge the dominant male agenda of specialised patriarchal language. One of the subtle yet effective challenges of feminist theologies is to speak in language that is accessible and, to a great extent, de-jargonized. This opens the whole theological realm to those who are 'non-specialist' and in so doing it breaks down the hierarchical game of knowledge possession that is so central to patriarchy. We must keep trying to find language that is even more accessible and remain unperturbed when our male colleagues therefore dismiss our work as lightweight and our concerns as lightweight.

Chapter 6

Sources for Theological Reflection

Feminist theology is a critique of the androcentric and misogynist views and judgments of patriarchal theology. As such it wants to reveal the authentic religious message 'as an authentic expression of the will of God' (Ruether 1987: 391). It is the response to and responsibility for God's call. In its response to that call it refuses to operate the old myopic mirror images of 'right' and 'left', of 'orthodox' and 'heretical', of 'traditional' and 'unacceptable' since these are the old method of confrontation and antagonism. New research in scripture studies, church history, systematic theology, missiology, anthropology, ethics and psychology combines in reformulating the way of doing theology. One of the most important components in this new way, as we have seen, is the bias towards women's experience in the expression of theology. Women's experiences beyond the biological experiences of menstruation, gestation, giving birth and lactation, women's experiences as 'critical experience of the devaluation of her person under patriarchal domination and her own journey of liberation' (Ruether 1987: 392) are recognized as a source for theological reflections.

When 'orthodoxy' is the overall concern, the narrow interpretation of what is right and what is wrong, it satisfies none but the most staid minds. Every generation has to interpret afresh, has to formulate new questions and find new answers. To allow no new investigations, to refer to answers frozen in time, is sterile. Thinkers are often attacked by the guardians of 'truth', by the ones who claim to have all the answers, for distorting reality, for an unhealthy preoccupation with aspects that they term marginal.

Feminist theology is a principle and a strategy guiding women and men to find and value the common and shared humanity in each other and to liberate each other from gender specific restrictions. Having critiqued it and demonstrated its flaws and bias, feminist theology is an offer to patriarchal theology, to take on board the holistic interpretation of inclusion. It is a critique of the impasse created by patriarchal theology. Elizabeth Moltmann-Wendel calls this exclusion of women the 'one-dimensionality of theology' (1986: 24). The Christian teaching of equality, always present since the beginning, but submerged under a one-sided exegesis, has together with other developments in society, surfaced in the last hundred years. A radical strand of Christianity has envisaged its goal to transform the existing structures of doing theology to become truly egalitarian.

Understood as a liberation movement, feminist theology has considerable political impact. The demand that everybody should be taken seriously, the demand to a right for personal development and autonomy, the demand to expand the radius of action for everybody so as to develop fully and find acceptance as a person and individual, have political consequences. They generated analysis and findings that question many an assumption in society and churches: our behaviour towards each other, the behaviour of states in the political arena and our attitude towards the exploitation of the earth's resources. A new paradigm of non-violence starting from our relationship of partnership with each other will issue in a major rethink of politics.

The tradition of exclusion is our tradition to date, but feminist theology sees tradition as 'a dynamic action of God's love which is to be passed on to others of all sexes and races' (Russell 1974: 79). To overcome the Christian praxis of exclusion means to shed the claim of patriarchal theology to speak for all and for all times. This step opens up a whole wealth of religious sources, previously termed 'heretical', as sources of equal importance (Pagels 1979). The task is to create a new relationship of equals, a gentle relationship with nature, enabling everybody to become an agent in his or her own right, with full personhood and autonomy, because by accepting divine revelation also in nature and in human interaction, in what we as women and men can experience, patriarchal Christianity may be pointed towards a transformation (Rouser 1990: 28-29).

Feminist theology has rejected the assumption of the sameness of human experience and of male values as normative values. Patriarchal prescriptions did away with doubt, the rationale for doubt was redacted out. This might have been an efficient method in times of little general education among laity and clergy, but now that women have equipped themselves with the tools for research and investigation, now that we are theologically literate, we find ourselves equipped to de-mask these prescriptions. Building on this insight women use their own experience as normative, and experience in all its diversity as normative. Scripture does speak of the different gifts of the faithful, but not neatly divided along gender lines. A division of labour—gifts, charisms, talents—along these lines is a falsification of the authentic religious message and part and parcel of the methods of the patriarchal system. A theology based on experience, though, faces the dilemma of a wealth of experience. What is normative and are there limits to accepting women's experiences as normative? It will be a major task to work out answers to these questions in the future. For the present the task it to learn to value difference. But as locus of revelation, of the meeting point with God and self, this difference will be seen as a reality to be celebrated and not eradicated. Feminist theology is therefore engaged in freeing women's potential from adapting to a system towards finding personal fulfilment, away from surviving a system towards living a faith.

Entering Eden with Eyes Wide Open

Where exactly should we start if we wish to critique patriarchal theology? How do we find the authority to carry out this task when we are so used to bowing to external authority and demands? We have seen that women's experience is a starting point but we do not become conscious of experience in abstracts, our experience lies in our concrete reality and this we grasp through our bodies. Our first task, then, in critiquing patriarchal theology is to reclaim the importance of our bodies. ' All that patriarchal culture has named evil must be reclaimed as part of ourselves—sensuality, change, darkness, self-affirmation, nature, death, passion, woman' (Brock 1988: 59).

The analysis of patriarchal culture by Brock gives us a framework in which to examine the issues of feminism more closely. This in turn sets the agenda for feminist theology if we position theology in the lived experience.

In reclaiming our bodies we are stating not only that the material, the physical, is a vehicle for the divine but that change is holy, that passion is sacred and self direction is the path of divinity. How different this is from the picture of Eve in Eden! Nature, the natural world, the creation in its totality is affirmed as sacred. Therefore when we as women claim our own bodies, not as objects to be harassed and mistrusted, but as sources of divinity to be freed and celebrated, we open up new realms in theology. This is where we start and where we should always return to find our motivation for doing theology. We should ask—what is happening to our bodies, the bodies of others and the body of the cosmos? If we see lack of love, nurture, respect and worship, then we must speak out; our critique is body-based and body-directed.

Feminist theologians such as Audre Lorde, Rita Brock and Carter Heyward explore this body-base of theology by declaring 'the erotic as power' (Heyward 1989: 87-118). Therefore, by claiming our bodies, we state that our physical nature is good and not shameful, we reclaim our power, the power we saw so neatly removed from the goddess in the patriarchal writing of the creation and fall. Patriarchy narrowed down the 'erotic' to the sexual, following the interpretation of the story of Eden. One result of this interpretation was that 'erotic' power was vilified, was regarded as insatiably lustful, as morally bad, ultimately as pornographic, without the realization that pornography is the exact opposite of the erotic since it is sensation without feeling, while the erotic feels deeply (Lorde 1984: 54).

The Greek word eros means love and is the name of the God of love, born of Chaos but personifying creative power and harmony. For Lorde and Heyward, the erotic is the assertion of the life force, it is empowering creative energy, 'the knowledge and use of which we are now reclaiming in our language, our history, our dancing, our loving, our work, our lives' (Lorde 1984: 55). Of course, women who come to such knowledge are thought of as dangerous! We are dangerous because our knowing goes deeper than mere intellectual assent and so it moves us to action. It does so from anger and from joy—from anger, because we realize how patriarchy has robbed us of our true being, how it has chained the truly creative power of human nature, how it has let destruction and separation rule when creativity and mutuality are our true nature; from joy, because once we feel it deeply within us, we know it is possible and so 'demand from ourselves and our life-pursuits that they feel in accordance with that joy which we know ourselves to be capable of' (1984: 57). We are touched so deeply that we need to seek that joy in the world. Therefore, claiming our bodies moves us away from abstract, otherworldly speculation and into the realm of concrete knowing and doing.

Once we move from the abstract to the embodied we open again the power of empathy and imagination. The latter was acknowledged long ago as necessary for people's survival, for a people without imagination perishes (Prov. 18). I know that if you cut me, I bleed, therefore I know you will; if you starve me, I die, therefore you will; if you beat me I feel pain, therefore you will. With no otherworldly speculation about holy suffering and reward we are spurred on to shout 'stop' for us—and for you. Once the body is perceived to be good, we are free to enjoy its pleasures and more: to grasp and practice the mutuality that it is capable of kindling in us in relationship with others. Once we feel this as creative spirituality and not as sin we want it for all people. Once our knowing is rooted deeply in our being, we cannot be silenced and we can no longer be insular and exclusive as patriarchy would wish us to be. Once we claim, in the language of Lorde and Heyward, the 'erotic' within us we are no longer powerless, because we are in touch with the creativity that is our true nature.

While acknowledging the 'erotic' as creative power and harmony, we should not lose sight of it being expressed sexually as well as in acts of more widely encompassing mutuality. Indeed, for Carter Heyward the 'erotic' is powerful in our most intimate sexual expression as much as in our global concerns, both the sexual act and the divine act of creation are 'empowering sparks of ourselves in relation' (1989: 3). Of course, both then need to be removed from the arena of 'power-over' to become vehicles of mutuality—empowerment. In our sexual relations we should not manipulate somebody else's feelings (Lorde 1984: 58) and in our religious quest we should not understand God as 'above and beyond', but as 'with us'. How we enter that relationship determines whether our lives and our world become creative, mutual and nurturing or destructive and alienating.

I Have Called you Friends (John 15.15)

It is very difficult for women to enter this world of mutual relation when we live in a reality that is so greatly influenced by patriarchy. Some women have been fortunate enough to find this mutuality with their partner; others have not. In her book *Fierce Tenderness: A Feminist Theology of Friendship*, Mary Hunt has developed a theology of friendship. She sees friendship as the model of healthy relating and the goal of human community (1991: 2). Friendship to her is theological because it not only means we are present and nurturing to one another but because we call forth the best from one another—our true friends challenge us and spur us on. If friendship is seen as a valid source of theological reflection, it implies new patterns of relating that reflect values of love and justice lived out between people (Hunt 1991: 14). If we dare to imagine an ethic based on friendship, Hunt claims there are far-reaching effects: images of the divine have to be rethought in the light of the fertile symbol system available in friendship; our relation to the earth has to be rethought in the light of mutuality; our view of church, society and even nuclear families have to be re-examined in the light of friendship (1991: 15).

The emphasis on friendship moves theology away from philosophy and the dualism it can neatly justify and into the realm of relationships and the complexities they present us with. Hunt claims she starts her theology 'with the data of real lives, people struggling to love well and act justly' (1991: 15). She makes the point that the emphasis on friendship is not over-personalizing theology or the transformation of patriarchy it envisages. Indeed, she says, feminist activists are finding that it is because of deeply rooted friendship that they are able to make social change in a patriarchal world (1991: 146). Friendship is not simply personal, it is political in that it gives root to and sustains the energies for change.

Mary Daly uses the idea of friendship when she explores what she prefers to call 'Be-friending' (Christ and Plaskow 1989: 199). This rather broadens the concept from personal involvement into a wider context. Daly is aware that not all feminists will be friendly with each other either because they do not know one another or indeed because of clashes in personality. However, we can all Be-friend one another, that is, we can 'weave a context in which women can Realize our Self-transforming, metapatterning participation in Be-ing. Therefore, it implies the creation of an atmosphere in which women are enabled to be friends' (1989: 200). She quotes Simone de Beauvoir's *The Second Sex* as an example: it created a climate in which women could relate to, and Be-friend, one another. It spurred women to action. In the same way women today who create 'women's space' either in politics, religion, the arts or personal relationships, are weaving a network of Be-friending. Women's space is a space in which women can learn to be self-affirming and creative away from the pressures of patriarchal society. Women's space is the arena of women's interaction, where the meeting of kindred spirits takes place; because it is women's space it is beyond competition and manipulation. Daly says women need this Be-friending 'both to sustain the positive force of moral Outrage and to continue the Fury-fuelled task of inventing new ways of living' (1989: 201).

Daly is not so naive to postulate that all women wish to Be-friend or be Be-friended; there are many women, who under the influence of patriarchy, oppress other women, races and classes. These women act as 'Rage-blockers/twisters' (1989: 203), who not only perpetrate patriarchy, but by so doing also discourage and confuse role models for other women for whom patriarchal politics appear of far greater importance. Daly points out that patriarchal politics of confrontation and aggression by their very nature frequently have catastrophic results. The logic of patriarchally conditioned women and men is hard to fault. Mass starvation or the threat of destruction of our biosphere would at first sight seem to place women's liberation somewhere down the list of priorities; once you realize, however, that all these issues are related and are all the result of dualistic thought patterns of conquest and submission, good and evil, them and us, you understand the very nature of patriarchy which exploits, disregards and destroys anything but itself. Modern patriarchs could be of any race and colour, of any social class. They could be middle-class fixers or military men who think the defence of the fatherland depends on them and warrants the destruction of the enemy within and outside. Or they could be leaders who have risen from humble origins of which they do not want to be reminded. As today it is often difficult to see beyond the immediate agenda of shoring up disaster, it is therefore the more important that women find a context in which to 'look beyond'. Precisely these actions of Be-friending, and solidarity because they are outside the control of patriarchy, are very frightening for patriarchy. We sometimes forget that models of victimization, be they racial, sexual or religious, were invented by patriarchy and that patriarchy requires the assimilation of women and, in Daly's words, 'our ghettoization from each other' (1989: 206).

Woman-to-Woman

Just how frightening women Be-friending one another can be is witnessed by the ridicule that men hurl at women who value their friendships with other women. Our communication is merely 'girls' talk' and not to be taken seriously. The ultimate verbal abuse is to label women as lesbians if we spend time valuing the company of other women. Due to the structures of society, such a label and the homophobia it carries with it, is enough to make many women shy away from contact with others and to make them reticent about their feelings. Feminism is interested in reclaiming lesbian experience because it is part of women's experience. Women's experience as the base of feminism is non-negotiable. Therefore, the whole range of experience must be included in the equation.

Charlotte Bunch advocates that the term lesbian should be used in a broader context than simply to denote a sexual relationship between women and should encompass all women who value women.

> A lesbian is a woman whose sense of self and energies, including sexual energies, centre around women—she is woman-identified. The woman-identified-woman commits herself to other women for political, emotional, physical and economic support. Women are important to her. She is important to herself. Despite the fact that our society demands that commitment from women be reserved for men (1987: 162).

This quotation shows why for Bunch a woman-to-woman relationship allows women to be fully committed to one another and that it does not draw them into patriarchy. It threatens patriarchy at large, it also threatens the religious structures because it places women's bodies outside the control of religious patriarchs. Such relationships declare that sexuality is good and positive for its own sake and not simply for procreation. Carter Heyward, a feminist, a lesbian, a Christian, defines same sex relationships as justice issues.

> Our passion as lovers is what fuels both our rage at injustice including that which is done to us—and our compassion, or our passion, which is on behalf of/in empathy with those who violate us and hurt us and would even destroy us (1989: 296).

The justice issue ultimately has a political potential: ' "I love you" means—let the revolution begin' (1989: 301).

According to Heyward, lesbianism is feared because it poses a threat to the nuclear family, the economic order, the gender of God, gender appropriate roles in work and at home, the norm of procreation, the sanctity of marriage and the acceptance of dominant-submissive relationships that are prevalent in all aspects of society (1989: 297). It dares threaten all these concepts, because it is the antithesis of patriarchy and it is patriarchy that justifies all the 'norms' just mentioned. While there was some apology for this position in the early days of lesbian theology, there is now a great celebration of it. It is much more clearly understood how the nuclear family and capitalism feed each other and lesbian liberation theologians would not wish to advocate anything that bolsters the genocidal reality of advanced capitalism.

It is clear from much of the rhetoric of the Christian Right in America that the family is viewed as pivotal in an agenda that goes far beyond individual morality and extends to economic and political power. It is in relation to this understanding that lesbian theologians are taking a stand. Rudy (1997) demonstrates how her experience as a lesbian theologian made her question the assumptions that come through when the Bible speaks of family and monogamy. She extends her analysis to say that in baptism we enter into a unitive relationship with a community and that this exceeds our experience of being gendered. While sex and orientation become less important according to her argument, hospitality and the corporate nature of our identity become more so. We are called to Christian hospitality and this can be expressed through any body and by any orientation. Hospitality calls us to be open and welcoming to all and it is this open heartedness that is the sign of a Christian and not matters of biology (Rudy 1997: 126). This does not gravitate towards marriage and indeed by following Rudy we could argue that by marrying and buying into the capitalist system we are exhibiting a great lack of hospitality to those who are most grievously exploited by the system.

Lesbian theologians stress friendship, be-friending and hospitality as ethics of commitment, as embodied life in all its diversity and this is a call for justice not simple hedonism. It poses questions for the concept of marriage and by implication calls into question the way we run society. It frees women to be-friend one another and is so doing allows greater freedom of expression for the self.

Pro-creation

It is, of course, true that not all feminists are lesbians and not all lesbians are feminists. But it was lesbians who brought the whole area of women's sexuality as something positive, which does not have to be connected with procreation, into the feminist debate. Ruether pointed out that women's procreative rights did not belong to her because 'the first subjugation of woman is the subjugation of her womb' (Ruether 1983: 260). Christian tradition has emphasized that a woman's body does not belong to her but to her husband and the fruit of her womb must belong to him also, hence the institution of marriage, prescriptions against adultery and chastity belts! Women have been told many things about their wombs, mostly based on wrong physiology (Ranke-

Heinemann 1990). First, that it is the passive receptacle of male power. Second, that original sin comes into the world through birth and so the womb is dirty. Birth, in fact, was considered so dirty that women had to be 'churched', had to be prayed over outside church after giving birth before being allowed back into God's house. For the child it is only the so-called second birth of baptism, administered by a man, that can cleanse it from the filth of the first birth from a woman's womb (Ruether 1983: 260). We have already seen the lengths to which the Church Fathers would go to sanitize Mary's womb and thereby Jesus' birth.

The sexual act outside a sacramentally blessed marriage has been forbidden as sinful. However, to prevent sperm from entering the womb, has been an ever greater sin within the Christian tradition. The Catholic church has declared contraception or masturbation a worse sin than rape, because both interfere with the sperm's divinely instituted destiny—the womb. During rape the sperm is not prevented from entering the womb (Borrowdale 1991: 99); it is held to be an act potentially creative and therefore abortion after rape is not permitted. The 1962 *Catholic Dictionary of Moral Theology* counsels women to accept the rapist and his act of utter invasion of body and mind. It declares that a woman can make reparation for being raped by marrying her rapist (Borrowdale 1991: 20). Why a woman should be counselled to make 'reparation' for violence done to her, is only understandable when one accepts the premise of patriarchy. From the same mind-set follows that if the sperm has been stopped by a barrier method of birth control, there can be no reparation. Such a ruling brutally reveals patriarchy. The harm done by a sexual act devoid of relationality and emotion is ruthlessly pushed aside and the woman, the rape victim, told to comply with the solution patriarchy offers her. Christian history, as Ruether so eloquently puts it, has given the message very plainly that woman 'must obediently accept the effects of these holy male acts upon her body, must not seek to control their effects, must not become a conscious decision maker about the destiny of her own body' (1983: 261).

The critique of patriarchy begins by reclaiming our bodies—understanding them as good and powerful. We now have to step out of the 'biology is destiny' model in a very positive way by declaring we are responsible for procreative choice. Beverley Harrison shows how far-reaching this decision is; it does not simply demand access to contraception but that the contraceptive methods available to us are safe. We have to ask detailed questions about women's health care in general (Andolsen, Gudorf and Pellauer 1985: 102). The questioning will no doubt result in inadequacies being uncovered; we already know that, for example, cancer screening is inadequate. It is by reclaiming our bodies that our action becomes political, such as when we ask how much money is spent on health care in comparison to military equipment.

Within the arena of procreative choice the issue of abortion is one that causes the greatest polarization. If the emphasis is always placed on the woman who chooses to end life, the very many 'cultural, social and economic consequences of pregnancy and childbearing' are not tackled (Andolsen, Gudorf and Pellauer 1985: 104). Abortion, or some of the reasons why women undergo abortions, are really social justice issues. To blame women by accusing them of using abortion as a method of contraception, is too easy.

Feminists need to ask is adequate safe contraception available, have women access to the economy in such a way as to support a child and does society give real choices about procreation? Women do not wish to have choice just for its own theoretical sake, but in order to exercise that choice practically for the greater moral good and more, to exercise that choice ourselves, not to have our rights defined for us. This alone signals a significant shift in society. The bearing and raising of children is, indeed, a very special task, perhaps the most special task; as such women must be in a position of decision making about it. Women must be sure of their willingness to undertake the task and we must demand that society supports us in that task. Instead of declaring that women who decide on abortion are in some way morally inadequate, we should ask how we can reduce the number. The answers will range from comprehensive sex education, which includes males taking responsibility to reducing sexual violence against women, as well as analysing the economics that make such choices necessary.

Sadly, the churches do not appear to be taking note of the feminist agenda in these areas of concern. Indeed, many churches of all shades of theology are retrenching when it comes to matters of women and our bodies. The most illuminating alliance between Roman Catholic and Moslem delegates at various UN conferences over the question of women's reproductive rights has been forged in the 1990s. That two such diverse religious groups, which on other occasions operate in opposition to each other, should stand together is a signal that patriarchies understand the importance of the control of women's bodies.

Another focus for feminist theology is that of IVF. While over-population is a strain felt in many countries, Westerners do not have their options for reproduction curbed but rather enhanced. The demands of childless couples have to be juxtaposed with the needs of global eco-logical concerns. However, there is not a great deal of guidance from the churches on these matters except to urge caution.

A Woman's Place...?

Lack of procreative choice had often served the purpose of confining the so-called 'kept' women to the home. It is often overlooked that working-class women and women of colour had little choice but to bear children and work outside the home as well as within. The work women do within the home is not classified as such, it is simply 'house-work' and 'wifely duties'. Women have traditionally provided a com-fortable and secure private sphere from which men go to make their mark on the 'real', public world. His achievements are noted in marble; hers are overlooked and taken for granted.

Women are not only denied self fulfilment outside the home but any work they do in the home has to conceal the ravages of toil—cosmetics, gentle detergents and so on help in this deception. The cosmetics industry has an annual turn-over of £20 billion while the diet industry tops it at £30 billion. The stakes have become even higher and women are not only able to have their faces, noses and breasts 'enhanced' they can now have 'designer genitals'. The rhetoric is that women should have their vaginas 'tidied up' to be more pleasing for their men. One American surgeon has already carried out in excess of 4000 such operations and reports that the men are pleased and the possibility of a vaginal orgasm is increased for the women (Cline 1994: 138). There is no consideration that sexual activity other than penetrative sex may be what women want, in other words the sex surveys that highlight the diffuse range of female sexual pleasure are overlooked in favour of male notions of sex. The woman undergoes the knife and patriarchy is satisfied in body and bank balance.

Woman is to be the beautiful house object, even down to her genitals. Indeed, a man's success is often measured by his ability to 'keep' a beautiful wife who he adorns with jewels and furs. It is this attitude of patriarchy that encourages men to take 'trophy wives' and display the young, beautiful women who look well in expensive clothes and jewellery. This, of course, leads to a number of middle-aged women being discarded by consumer patriarchy. When a woman becomes a sign of male affluence she plays a game that not only diminishes her but also places other women, in less affluent households, at risk. The 'home' becomes yet another area of patriarchal hierarchy, mirroring public life where power is dispensed by those with authority, usually men.

Those women who attempt to run a family and go out to work without outside assistance are often criticized for not being competitive enough in the work place. The question is not asked whether family labour should be divided so as to allow women to stay on at the office and discuss developmental plans, rather than having to rush off to shop and have a meal ready when the partner returns (Ruether 1983: 262). The myth that it is best to be at home, in the private, quasi cloistered sphere, tending their man, is something many women wish to explode. They want to work outside the home and find fulfilment in their work and by doing so claim their selfhood, challenge economics and misogyny. A woman who insists on adequate care for her children while she works is expensive and poses political questions.

While more women work there does not appear to be a change in what they are expected to do at home. Women are feeling depressed and view themselves as failures while men are priding themselves on their new man status. The extra work load for women does not mean that they will gain the promotion or be awarded the salaries that they deserve and so the trap seems to have widened. There is a crisis for women (Greer 1999). The Labour government in the UK, of whom one would have expected more, is urging single mothers to go back to work in order to reduce the benefits budget, but the jobs available are limited and limiting. There is no real attention given to job share or child care provision at high standards and low cost. The churches are not quick to provide for these needs—why not? In short, yet another no win situation for women.

However, the home is not a safe place for women, with two women a week being killed by their partners or ex-partners. This is a shocking reality but also one that is not addressed by the churches. Children are also at risk. While we may think it can get no worse many sociologists warn that the crisis of masculinity that seems to be sweeping Britain and America will only add to the rates of violence towards women. The scapegoating, so eloquently started with the Eden story, continues and women pay very heavily for it—at times with their lives.

Some Girls Do...!

There are some women who are at home in the public sphere, on street corners, on Page Three or in blue movies. These women know their place; it is in any position that pleases men. Feminism has often been accused by anti-feminists of prudery, of spoiling fun, of having no humour, of ranting. If women want to engage in the 'oldest' profession, let them! After all, they do no harm, nobody forces them, and they make a handsome profit. It is even said that they keep the child molesters and perverts away from respectable women and children and society should therefore be grateful to prostitutes, pin-ups and pornography. Accepted wisdom is that it is the 'unfeminine' women, who fail to attract men, who want to spoil their fun and who turn into strident feminists to get back at the men.

The argument that women who engage in prostitution do no harm overlooks the whole issue of the harm that is done to women. Their emotional needs are not met, while their body is exploited. The argument, that nobody forces a woman into prostitution is plainly naive, since the majority of women engaged in prostitution are driven into it by the most dire necessity. The handsome profit is handsome only for a very small group of women. The majority are governed by pimps who take the profit, while the rest sell themselves for food for their children. And as to the 'oldest' profession, it is debatable that it is, since it is a by-product of patriarchy and its injunctions on virginity for the married women, and patriarchal property rights. An attack in the media on the expert writer on pornography, Andrea Dworkin, reasoned that she disliked pornography because she was ugly.[1]

Due to the spread of AIDS there has been a global call for prostitutes to be younger and younger. The male logic appears to be that the younger they are the less likely they are to be infected! In places like Thailand this has led to an already young population of prostitutes having their ages reduced yet again. It is not unusual for village girls as young as five to be taken from their homes, either sold by male relatives or kidnapped (Brock and Thistlethwaite 1996).

The 'sex industry' is worth some £17 billion a year in Britain alone, yet we do not see a large number of female millionaires, who have made a fortune from their bodies. We learn that in Asia the sex industry was

---

1.   *The Sun* (20 October 1991).

planned as a development strategy and backed by the World Bank, the IMF and the United States Aid for International Development Fund (Brock and Thistlethwaite 1996: 114). Asian women and children are provided on the cheap for Western men. Such development plans related to countries where the people are not white raises another level of concern. The sex industry not only operates from a level of deep hatred for women but also carries with it higher than average levels of racism. It is naive to think that while 'working women' are being used as objects through the sex industry then 'decent women' are being spared the same treatment. Once the mindset of objectification exists we can all fall prey to it.

Because feminist theology starts from human experience and because it argues for a new understanding of our bodies as whole and not deficient, as sacred, and not sinful, it moves the debate on prostitution and pornography away from 'good' and 'bad' and into the realm of blasphemy and exploitation. It examines the whole question of how women are viewed in society. The morally questionable issue of Page Three girls is not that they show naked flesh to a wide audience, but by so doing they encourage women to be seen as objects. Men are enabled by constant exposure to such material to alienate themselves from women. The smiling face on Page Three makes no demands of the men who desire the body; the message is 'If you are happy, I am happy'. Any suggestion of relationship is totally absent. As such, the picture is pornographic, because it is alienating and asymmetrically power-laden. It is not mutually empowering, an expression of creative energy, the divine.

As feminist theologians we need to question pornography and prostitution at their roots, which are financial. Many men make fortunes out of female flesh and women have no choice but to sell their bodies in this way. The whole topic becomes more disturbing with the statistic that 90 per cent of women in prostitution and pornography have been abused as children (Borrowdale 1991: 84).

Pornography is not erotic sex, it is not empowering, it is controlling and dominating. Men are in charge and women are delighted by it. Or so the porn films will have us believe, when they show women who are being gang raped enduring their ordeal smilingly (Borrowdale 1991: 82). Borrowdale believes it is no accident that the porn industry is on the increase at a time when women are demanding equal rights with men (1991: 88). Pornography enables men to feel power over women; the Hite report found that many men think of sex as a weapon with which to hurt and punish women and regard rape as a way of putting women in their place (Borrowdale 1991: 88).

Pornography needs to be challenged as blasphemy. The pornographic mind is at work whenever 'men assume the right to buy women, or control their lives, whenever women are subordinated to men' (Borrowdale 1991: 91). Our resistance to pornography stems from our hope to free 'erotic' power, not to limit it to genital sex. A partnership that is truly erotic leads to the desire to relate and to find pleasure with one another. It does not find pleasure through violence and dominance. In questioning the use of women's bodies in pornography we are not asking for censorship but for a different portrayal of relationships. Women's bodies are not for sale in the market place of dominance and submission. Our bodies are vehicles of joy and relationship. Sexual lust is not wrong; alienating and objectifying the recipient of one's sexual lust *is* wrong.

For the everyday language associated with sex, we need new expressions just as much as we do for other areas of life. Mary Hunt suggests the use of the term 'mutual pleasuring', while Carter Heyward refers to 'embodied justice seeking' (1989: 10). The language needs to reflect the acknowledgement that our bodies are ours to give freely in mutual ecstatic equal relation.

The Earth, our Sister

In stark contrast to the alienation and objectifying that pornography encourages, Susan Griffin is able to experience the sacred through the passionate connection with the whole of nature (Christ and Plaskow: 105-10). The interdependence, mutual respect and nurture of love and nature take the place of dominance and submission. She makes the connection of partnership between equals, between friends and between people and the life sustaining earth.

Hunt argues that friendship kindles kinship, connection with people and nature, an 'ecofeminism'. 'Ecology is the act of befriending the earth and its inhabitants, guaranteeing for future generations access to the natural world that we have enjoyed' (1991: 84). Thus our friendship connects past and future generations.

Ruether also sees a link between the disregard with which people treat people and the disregard with which people treat the earth. She puts it forcefully by stating: 'Through the raped bodies, the earth is raped' (1983: 263). Patriarchy, and its economic system of exploitative individual and state capitalism, thrives on dominance and this is extended to the earth and its resources. Patriarchy will take what it wants because it considers its needs to be supreme. Even the text of patriarchy, in this case the book of Genesis, commands such an attitude by saying: 'Be fruitful and multiply and fill the earth and subdue it and have dominion over the fish of the sea and over the birds of the air and over every living thing that moves upon the earth' (Gen. 1.28). This exposes the text as patriarchal propaganda if we understand it against the background of the goddess religion and, furthermore, it suggests that 'to subdue' is to exploit; it does not suggest 'to subdue' means to restrain in order to cultivate. The result of this attitude is that we are running after more profits, while the ever more finite resources of the earth are depleted. Little thought is given to this fact, as we have accepted the view that humanity has the right to treat nature in this manner.

When one acknowledges mutuality and interdependence, then the whole world view is shifted. Some feminist theologians invest goddess religion, which is held to be non-hierarchical, with the paradigm of mutuality and connectedness. The world must be valued, because it is the body of the goddess. Starhawk shows the emphasis of goddess religion by saying:

> The image of the Goddess strikes at the root of estrangement. True value is not found in some heaven, some abstract other world, but in female bodies and their offspring, female and male; in nature; and in the world. Nature is seen as having its own inherent order, of which human beings are a part (1988: 10).

She declares the notion, prevalent in Christianity, that nature is fallen and our ultimate goal is to distance ourselves from it, null and void. For her the importance is firmly on involvement. It is also on cause and effect; if we abuse the earth, we will suffer, the just and the unjust alike. If we spray forests with mutagenic chemicals, there will be miscarriages and birth defects once the chemicals get into the water supply. If we store nuclear waste in dangerous ways, cancer will be more prevalent in people (Andolsen, Gudorf and Pellauer 1985: 195).

As life is sacred, it demands our full active participation, which in itself requires our commitment to justice. There is no external God to guarantee salvation to the 'chosen', when there is a nuclear leak even the 'chosen' develop cancer. Consequences are suffered collectively and so it is our collective responsibility to transform society and the practices that destroy lives and the interplay of life forms around us (Andolsen, Gudorf and Pellauer 1985: 199). We change it by participating in it in a justice seeking way. Our survival requires that we refrain from plundering finite resources or we will destroy the earth, the life-force, which is the goddess. The message is plain, the penalty is fatal.

Despite the gravity of the situation many Christian theologians are slow to engage with the matter of ecology. Anne Primavesi, calls for a real relationship with Christ in the created order, which requires political action rather than awe and mystical wonder. She understands the whole world to be an ecological community, one that is held together by the realities of process thought and the cosmic Christ. These two concepts highlight what she considers to be self evident truths, that salvation is a process that requires all to be saved or none are saved (1991: 151).

In her book *Women Healing Earth* (1996) Ruether demonstrates just how much political action is needed. The book contains articles by third world women who graphically illustrate the concrete effects of lack of ecological regard on their lives and those of their families. They are not merely inconvenienced by the way the West acts, they are in fact placed in risk and often pay with their lives. Such a reality calls for action that will change the way the world is, it calls for people of good will to place pressure on the governments of the West who are the greatest offenders against the ecological balance.

All this is very cerebral and in the opinion of McFague (1993) can leave room for inaction. For her, the first crucial step towards a workable ecotheology is to come out of our heads and into our bodies. It is in this stuff of matter that we are really grounded in the earth and from there we can begin to understand the problems and find grounded solutions (1993: 2-3). Once we really appreciate that we emerged from the same one millioneth of a gram of hot matter as the rest of the planet then we will, in McFague's opinion, be obliged to give up any grandiose ideas about stewardship and subduing the earth—these are pure fantasy. We also come to realize that the earth has subjectivity just as we have and so we are able to cast a loving eye over it. That is, an eye that allows everything its place and dignity in its place (1993: 34). In urging us to go back to our roots and have close encounters with the earth McFague is hoping that we will touch and see the 'aliveness' of all matter and thus come to nurture it more.

Ecofeminist theologians are gradually realizing that the earth is not a moral issue tagged on the end of Christian doctrine. The whole question of ecofeminism raises questions about co-creation and co-redemption. It was, at one time, assumed that notions of co-creation and co-redemption applied only to the human inhabitants of the planet and did not touch the non-human inhabitants and the planet itself. Of course, when metaphysical notions are challenged as strongly as they are by feminist theology it is not surprising that the questions of where creation and redemption are to take place are soon asked.

Ivone Gebara (1999) illustrates that ecofeminist theology challenges not only capitalism, in other words, the way we choose to understand money, but also all forms of knowledge and even the definitions we hold dear about the human person. All have to be re-thought if we take the earth seriously as our sister in creation and redemption. Our frames of reference are no longer Thomist and Platonic but rather the entire material world and all its inhabitants. Gebara not only highlights the challenges but to an extent shows how meeting these challenges has been inhibited by Christian theology. Having set out a very exciting and relevant agenda, Gebara reverts to the Trinity, Jesus and God as the way to fully explore her insights. The inevitable happens. Many of the 'answers' are predictable and we are still screened from the reality of nature by the trinitarian energy we are told it holds and we should embrace. The mindset of Christianity inhibits the creativity of the engagement.

Nevertheless Gebara alerts us to the fact that women and nature are both used as weapons of war. This is an insight that has not been developed by other ecofeminist theologians and is one worth pondering. Women are raped and beaten in order to witness to the power of the aggressor and nature is polluted and ravaged as a reminder of the cost of defeat. Many years after the Gulf War there has still not been a clean-up operation, with the result that the numbers of cancer victims have risen beyond imagination. Depleted uranium used to coat the tips of bombs is in the atmosphere and being ingested by all who are unfortunate enough to live in the vicinity. Many are paying the price long after the conflict is over.

Despite drawing our attention to dire realities Gebara is still sure that there is a way to relate to the earth that can bring about both its flourishing and our own. Grace Jantzen draws our attention to the fact that 'flourishing' is a well chosen term in feminist theology, as in Latin the noun is feminine and of course the word means to bloom and grow vigorously (Isherwood and McEwan 1996: 70-72). Jantzen suggests that a theology of flourishing is much better than one of salvation which tends to imply that we have to be rescued from something by somebody. Flourishing, on the other hand, suggests an internal dynamic that is good, abundant and productive. Jantzen hopes to reimage the connection between women and nature as a positive one through an emphasis on flourishing. A knock-on effect will be that men, if they are to be understood as good, will also have to renew their relationship with the earth rather than with the spiritual realm.

Jantzen highlights how by starting with the earth and a model of flourishing we also move away from an individualistic view of salvation (Isherwood and McEwan 1996: 71). To think in terms of the individual in relation to such a model is to reduce it to the absurd. Of course, once we are called to think in terms of the whole we find that questions of North/South, developed/developing world enter the equation. If all are to flourish then capitalism as much as individual goodness is on the agenda. We are no longer saved from the world but plunged more deeply in it, to root and to flourish. Jantzen, like Gebara and McFague, shows that we are of the earth and it is only in a positive engagement with it that we will make possible a just and open future.

Once feminism declares that the body is a resource for the creation of theologies a wide vista is opened up before us. Theology ceases to be the cerebral activity of chosen men and becomes a lived enactment of all who live and breathe. The discipline has been criticized for emphasizing the body as such a resource when it is pointed out that not all people experience empowerment in their bodies. It is true that there was an initial exuberance about the joys of placing the body in the realms of theological exploration but this has since been tempered by the testimonies of the differently abled and those who find their bodies to be sites of suffering for any number of reasons. However, the body still remains a fundamental site for theological reflection even if our optimism has to be restrained. It also becomes an enacted ethical imperative when we realize that much of its suffering has been caused by pollution, war, capitalism and other results of patriarchy.

The earth itself having been ignored for centuries of Christian history is once more taking centre stage and posing the kinds of questions that we cannot afford to ignore. There is a danger, of course, that it will be no more than an object in this new enthusiasm to be ecologically sound. However, feminist thinkers are aware of the dangers and are encouraged and challenged by the possibilities that open up before them for new ways of thinking and being. By starting from experience in the creation of theology feminism has been able to offer as resources those things that have been abused over the centuries by a thoroughly dualistic and metaphysical scheme. We are far from exhausting those theological resources yet even now we see that the dominant discourse can never again be the same.

Chapter 7

The Vision of a New Beginning

Feminist theology demands a radically different interpretation of scripture and tradition in view of the millennia old oppressions of women. At the beginning of a new millennium oppression and discrimination have no future. A colonial mind-set that knows everything better than others and acts on what it knows can no longer be tolerated. By demanding another future feminism critiques patriarchy but feminism itself is not above reproach. We have come a long way in uncovering the creeping myopia of patriarchy in religion and we have challenged many areas of androcentric thinking but we were slow to realize that there is not one feminist theology but many. Even in our efforts not to dogmatize there have tended to be 'right ways' of seeing things. This book has attempted to be as inclusive as possible; however, it does acknowledge that its breadth is limited by the experience of the authors; we are white, middle-class academics. Still the summary provides clues for those who wish to engage more critically with the Western tradition of Christianity in the hope of finding a more wholesome future for the planet and those who inhabit it. Such an approach will always appear as unscholarly or as 'messy' because we are so used to the clear lines of demarcation that doctrine and tradition have always used as the boundaries between the heretic and the believer. No such lines are drawn in feminist theologies. The academic discipline we know as feminist theology is very young and so we should expect that it has made and will make mistakes. We may even expect that its progress appears slow, but then Christianity has taken 2,000 years to move as far as it has.

We are still very much at the beginning, perhaps the end of the beginning, of this new process. The new way of questioning is still startling to many and the churches have not even begun to engage with the methods and critiques of feminist theologies. However, feminist theology has placed gender on the map. The philosopher Charlotte Perkins

Gilman speaks of two different focal points for male and female religious experiences arising from the life experience of man the hunter and woman the nurturer. Male religion to her is a religion of death and the obsession with what comes after death:

> To the death-based religion, the main question is 'What is going to happen to me after I'm dead?—a posthumous egoism. To the birth-based religion the main question is 'What is to be done for the child that is born?'—an immediate altruism... The death based religions have led to a limitless individualism, a demand for the eternal extension of personality... The birth-based religion is necessarily and essentially altruistic, a forgetting of oneself for the good of the child,and tends to develop naturally into love and labor for the widening range of family, state and world (1923: 46-47).

To pursue the ideal of immortality is no pursuit for feminist theologies (Isherwood and Stuart 1998). The discussion of immortality centres on the faulty interpretation of patriarchal religion, with all its mechanisms of oppression, discrimination and its linear way of salvation in history which issues in 'universal imperialism' (Ruether 1983: 250) This discussion stresses the life-sustaining nurture and love and care. However, we need to avoid the trap of nurturing to the exclusion of ourselves. Love and care have also been traps well laid for women, many have extinguished themselves in the living out of both.

Are we perhaps in danger of polarizing the debate too much, can we really operate in what at times seems to be dangerously like an essentialist argument? The easy answer to this is that we all have unique situations in the world, which will affect the way we see things. Women have not had their experiences included in religious reflection but have had their situations prescribed. We should then, perhaps not be too surprised that talk of nurture, love and care are on the agenda as this is what we have been encouraged to do. As we reflect more on what it is to be a woman, the debate from experience will not all be about nurture and care; it will include a wider range of experience for reflection. However, that does not deal with the question of whether there are some experiences that women have that men can never have. There are exciting new developments in the neurological field (although we have of course to be cautious about embracing them), but they do suggest that women have far greater 'thinking matter' and are able to utilize both sides of the brain at once. This will inevitably mean that we experience the world differently from men and perhaps it is time to state boldly that this opens up a wider vista of knowledge. Perhaps essentialism has a point!

If this is the case does it follow that images of the divine will be split into male and female and that such a split could lead away from male monotheism to polytheism? Perhaps this does not matter, as indeed it does not to some pagans and goddess worshippers. However, from a Christian perspective such a view seems intolerable. Indeed, the whole question of the gender of God is a sticky one for some Christian theologians. While it is by no means solved for those who are feminist theologians. The question of inclusion and valuing of the female is not simply solved by changing the gender of God. What we could end up with is God in a frock, which will be of no ultimate good to anyone. What has to change is our perception of what the divine is like as well as our understanding of the power relation between the divine and creation. A great all-powerful father replaced by a great all-powerful mother does not alter the theological landscape sufficiently for a new way of being to emerge. Likewise a recourse to goddesses and goddess worship, supposed to be the norm before patriarchy and patriarchal religions, would not open up a passable way for transforming Christian scriptures and worship.

Feminist theologies understand themselves as non-authoritarian and this requires that the concept of deity gives up hierarchical power and authority. This places responsibility squarely in the hands of the believers. Feminist theologians are either accused of being too idealistic, holding ideas that can never come to fruition, or conversely not being idealistic enough. The latter is usually in relation to questioning metaphysical hopes. The former is usually countered with 'face the facts' exercises, such as a reminder about the realities of global capitalism and the power of multinational companies. Nevertheless, it is crucial that we should not give up on utopian dreams. Humans have always derived a great deal of energy from the myths and dreams they project into the world. Roughly speaking the process at work is one of hope, aspiration, projection and inspiration. It appears that humans have difficulty with being inspired by their own aspirations and have instead to place them in the hands of God to be legitimized. Feminist theologies are questioning the safety of the hands of God; the old myths have to go but where is the inspiration now? Goddess women find this in the re-membering of the tales of the goddess while those who are non-realist remain at a loss or place meaning in the body and the interrelationships between bodies and the earth. It does not have to be this way. Utopian dreams/ visions do not have to work as paralysers as Christian eschatology has, they can instead remind us of the reality we strive for and spur us into creatively achieving that goal. In order to avoid imagining that there is one universal and infinite vision, at the very least feminist theologies have to embrace the reality of change. As quantum theology grows and develops it appears there could be very many points of creative interaction between it and feminist theologies. Unlike patriarchal theology, feminist theology, does not see any development of chaos theory as a threat but rather as a very welcome ally against the rigid categories of patriarchal control.

Feminist theologies are sometimes accused of denying the existence of sin and destruction. This is a wrong understanding: feminist theology denies the link that is usually made between sexist stereotypes of evil and female. Faith is not an act of obedience without growth of one's own power. Faith is not a question of either/or, sinner/penitent, but a question of gradual growth to the whole experience of faith (Halkes 1985: 44), a long process, an event of communication with others and nature and God. The split between heaven and earth in patriarchal theology cannot accommodate what feminist theology describes as a holistic process of salvation, starting with the here and now. The argument is that it would allow syncretism to creep into theological orthodoxy and would present the danger of making God part of nature, his creation. This bias is not shared by feminist theology, as we are not afraid of getting in touch with nature and renaturalizing the world. Feminist theologies, along with other liberation theologies, prefer to understand sin and destruction as material realities rather than metaphysical states. Concrete realities require concrete actions to overcome them and this is certainly sought from those who call themselves liberation/feminist theologians. Due to denial of destructive dualism feminist theologies are left to face destructive edifices like global capitalism or state communism. In the face of global poverty at a level we have never experienced bishops in the United Kingdom seem to be more concerned about the abolition of Section 28 of the Local Government Act, which bans the promotion of homosexuality in schools, and about restating marriage as the only legitimate form of relationship between humans. This is an expression of theological practice which wishes to control people rather than make the world a better place.

Feminists are slow to declare acts of love between consenting adults to be sinful but quick to point out the destructive nature of patriarchal edifices, in this case the teaching on marriage. They are wrong because they are attempting to perpetuate a system that is destructive. This highlights the difference between a feminist approach to sin and that of patriarchal theology. How the world looks as a result of our actions is of prime importance. This does not mean that the end justifies the means but rather that matters of sin and destruction have a far more material sense about them than they have had to date. To take the notions of sin and destruction into the political realm and keep them there is of prime importance to feminist theologians.

The Sermon on the Mount still remains a strong call to morality but is viewed as a call to world peace, not just inner peace, as well as full human rights. The latter means that feminist theologies need to stand firm against any demonization of persons according to gender, colour, class or orientation. Metaphysics in the realm of sin and morality can lend itself to the creation of demons while a solid materialist approach looks at structures and the way in which they can be turned to the good. This is not to deny the place of individual sin but rather to acknowledge that in the world in which we live vast numbers of good people do bad things because of the grip of structures on their lives. There is always individual moral choice but this, like democracy needs to be learned and practised, a process that is getting harder and harder under the weight of global markets and multinational companies. Feminist body theologians are perhaps those who hold out the greatest hope for individuals to learn to differentiate and nuance and so to turn around the huge weight of modern economic systems. While they are the first to acknowledge that the individual body like everything else is constructed by the system, they also understand that the body can act in transgressive and transformative ways. This, after all, is the central message of Christianity, a religion with incarnation at its heart (Isherwood and Stuart 1998).

Feminist theologians are sometimes critiqued for putting too much emphasis on bodily self-identification. Indeed, this is a criticism not just from those outside the discipline but by some within it. Many women in theology from contexts other than the West find that identifying with the body is not necessarily a good experience or a liberating one. This would be particularly true in countries where there are high rates of child prostitution or sex tourism. The kind of body identification that some Western theologians pursue would not be helpful in these situations. Further, there are many women Buddhist scholars for whom an entirely different set of understandings operate in relation to the body. What we come to realize is that the body is far more than a set of physical components; it is a cultural construct and therefore has to be engaged with as such. The body is the first place that discrimination is played out. We may not do this or that because of the particular body we have, we will be perceived in certain ways because of the body we possess. Apartheid, sexism, able-bodiedness, homophobia and many more all operate on the level of assessing and judging bodies and their actions. Surely, then, this is a good place to challenge the ideology and present the body as a cultural icon of another and more inclusive set of principles and lived realities. Christianity thrives on the memory of the resurrection of the body and the new world order it was meant to signify: Christians then should not be afraid to use their bodies as new order signifiers.

While emphasizing bodies feminist theologies have been accused of down-playing the central importance of one body, the body of Christ and they have also been accused of relativizing the importance of Jesus by seeing God's power only in relation to human, social and societal and natural experiences. Indeed, this is one of the criticisms that Daphne Hampson offers when she argues that Christianity is no longer viable. For her (1990) Christianity says something about the nature of Jesus rather than simply making ethical statements about him. Christianity operates in the realm of essences not just ethics. It is for this reason and in the light of modern science that Hampson finds the Christian project no longer tenable. However, she also feels that it is not ethical enough either. Nevertheless she has little sympathy with those, even feminists, who wish to 'lower' christology in the hope of saving Christianity.

It is certainly true that many feminist theologians do not wish to assert the once and for all sacrifice of the only son of God as the central understanding of the place of Jesus in the Christian tradition. However, this is not just from a mere whim but is a position based both on historical and psychological considerations. It is unquestionably true that christology, how Jesus has been understood, has never been a static doctrine and the differences have not always divided heretics from believers. The mainstream of the church has often changed its mind. It is also true to say that what we believe affects us. Many women have not found a place for themselves in the main stream christologies which on the whole are outworkings of dualistic metaphysics and the alienations that such views bring in their wake. Encouraged by the promise of equality and salvation that they received in baptism many women went in search of a more inclusive and woman friendly Jesus.

There is now a whole array of feminist Christs just as there were patriarchal ones before. Under the weight of experience of women from around the world the Christ figure has enlarged and blossomed. He is no longer the colonial face of conquest and cultural genocide in Asia but is the woman shaman, the healer, the grain of rice and the soother of han, the suffering of the people. In India Christ represents Shakti, the innate divine energy, and is seen by some as the menstrual blood of the struggling, birthing women—struggling to birth a just society and one that values their bodies. In Latin America, as well as being a brother in the struggle, Christ is also imaged as a young prostitute being raped by men in public toilets. In the West Christ is the liberator, the example of erotic connection, the healer, the one who stands in solidarity. For some Africans Christ is the cosmic redeemer. The black and Womanist Christ is black in a world that values whiteness and is the constant hope of a new morning, a new dawn when value is in the person and not in the colour (Isherwood 1999).

Despite these different stresses there is still a question mark and that is around the power that this reimaged Christ may still hold in the world. For those like Hampson the question of feminist autonomy and Christian submission is one that will not go away. She argues that however this Christ may look there is still a point at which we give ourselves to him and this flies in the face of feminist autonomy.

The power of Christ has in the West been less a question of the way in which those 'in Christ' may make the world a better place and more about how they may make it their own through conquest and latterly through the exercising of 'superior moral judgments'. This is a trap that feminist theology must avoid—while the former is not a real consideration the latter can become a temptation. There is a balance to be struck between annunciating a liberating vision and declaring it to be the true way. This is keenly highlighted in feminist ethics as much as in the christological debates. There is a long way to go yet in terms of the 'power of Christ' debate and it will be interesting to see how it develops over the years. Will there be a discipline called feminist christology or will the taking of one's own power have eliminated the necessity for such a discussion?

Many feminist theologians embrace postmodernism as a useful travelling companion, since it questions all metanarratives, as feminists have been doing for many centuries, and works in limited truth claims. However, as we have seen, it is reluctant to place one moral claim above another. Can feminist theology really go along these lines? We go so far but then we have to call a halt, there is still a 'so far and no further' line in the sand for feminist theology—although we will all differ as to where it is. Liberative and justice seeking action has to be the base line and behind that the debate still carries on. Feminist theologians are adamant that the political edge in the discipline must not be lost, the point is to make the world a better place not just to talk about it. This means politics in the world in which we live, engagement with the realities of life and concrete action for change. We live in exciting times.

There are those who feel that feminist theology has not delivered 'the goods', that it has promised a great deal and achieved very little. From a standing start feminist theology has developed hermeneutical disciplines, ethical disciplines, recovered women in history that were either unknown or greatly misrepresented, pushed for ordination, given women back a sense of the goodness of the body, delved into multiculturalism and postcolonial discourse in a way that patriarchy has yet to appreciate. It has also opened up worship and many more forms of spirituality, it has taken seriously the pagan traditions and embraced the positive nature of goddess religion. It has opened up new branches of theology such as ecotheology and has engaged with psychology of religion in a very productive and inspiring way. The philosophy of religion can no longer pretend that the world is white and male and language is under scrutiny in a way previously unknown. It has challenged governments over nuclear issues, sex tourism and globalization as well as challenging individuals over sexism, racism and homophobia. It has seen the link between the various forms of oppression in a way not done to date and it will not allow homophobia to be the last acceptable form of prejudice. It has done and is doing much more and all this in 30 years. What basis is there for the claim that feminist theology has been disappointing? There are still glass ceilings for women at work but they are now more visible than they were before. This does not make it better but it does make resistance more possible, we can fight what we can see. Not even the most unenlightened individual or institution can claim it has not heard that women are ready, capable and willing to engage in all strands of employment in a constructive and creative way. Feminisms of all shades have taken away the excuses that polite males used to keep women out of the systems. The churches may no longer claim that they know nothing of inclusive language or that there were no female prophets. They cannot claim neutrality in scriptural reading or job prospects for women clergy. Our expectations of them to act morally and mindfully are huge advances.

Yet there is still a great deal to be cleared away; many more women need to be recovered, and celebrated, from the rubble of patriarchal theology. The world of male centred philosophy needs to be by-passed in the creation of woman centred epistemologies. There are new technologies that impact on all lives, but most often on the lives of women, to be engaged with and challenged. We still need safe and affordable contraception and women's health programmes that value equally women's and men's bodies. Global economics need to focus to a far greater extent on women and children.

The very varied and rich strands of which we have spoken explore a whole range of aspects of feminism and their impact on feminist theology. Our critique of patriarchy, which begins with our experience of owning our bodies and the power that lies within them, takes us into the realms of politics, church structure, doctrine and societal norms and expectations. The vision of feminist theology is a world where individual dignity and integrity are honoured in mutual relating, where the life giving power replaces the life denying power and people are enabled to accept their humanity joyfully.

We have no wish to make this sound like a static feminist utopia. All things change and it is the positive nature of change that feminist theologians wish to uphold. They have no prescriptions for absolute results but rather a commitment to the process of each person's becoming. The structures envisaged need to free people and not impose exploitation on resources, human and non-human. This is not simply a human vision, but because it is a human vision it is a divine vision; the concept of heaven has been moved from above-and-beyond and placed in the lived experience of real people and their real lives. Our commitment to the dismantling of patriarchy stems from our understanding that patriarchy is not bad because we as women do not have the upper hand within it; patriarchy is bad because it divides the world, creation, into a rigid two-caste system. The hierarchy of dominance and submission that is its basic premise stretching from the divine to the non-human realms has caused endless suffering and could, we believe, bring ultimate destruction. By demanding an end to sexism we claim once again our own power and we are also claiming a future for the planet. We stand against the sin of sexism because of the destructive value system it represents. By valuing ourselves as women, we are not selfish, we bring our gifts to the world.

'The Gods have only observer status' writes Berthold Brecht in his play *The Good Person of Sechuan*. The gods (and the patriarchs ruling in their names) have a privileged position from which to observe and judge. The rough and tumble of life does not touch them. They are outside and beyond human experience. The Christian message, however, is that God is with us, precisely located in the rough and tumble of human life. Christianity has made God accessible to humanity, experienceable in the ups and downs of human life. God is compassionate, is with us, is in the middle of our struggle. To codify what we as humans have to think about God is to undervalue our own struggle to find God and to give rigorous interpretation of how we ought to envisage 'Him'. Although patriarchal theology is at pains declaring God not experienceable with our sense apparatus, because God is outside human limits of gender and sex, patriarchal theology is happily using human similes that firmly ground God as a male person. And, to use Mary Daly's phrase, 'if God is male, then male is God'. The subjection of females under the control of the males is validated by a theology thinking God as male. It is this rigid interpretation that dislocated our understanding of God. In rigid formulas there is no possibility for change. In compassionate trust there is possibility for change.

We have dared to pose the question of conscious dissent. 'Where am I in my relationship with God?' is the far deeper concern than 'Do I follow all the rules and regulations of patriarchy?' Critical questioning is the leaven of intellectual debate. If we do not engage in such questioning, patriarchal theology will suffer from academic rigor mortis. The exodus of theology from academe is a fact just as much as the welcome theology is given in the lives of ordinary people who want to do theology. They know about their own values and want to build on them. The new way, the feminist way, of pluralism and lived experience, of individual worth and collective responsibility, is like new wine in old skins. Equality and justice were the two radical commitments of the nascent Christian community in the time of apostles. Hierarchy and dominance were the two radically different results of established Christianity. The first strand, though, never really was lost, albeit buried and forgotten from time to time. There were always believers who never lost sight of the Christian message of 'love one another'. And thus Christianity was able to overcome culturally defined stereotypes, most of all racism.

It is our belief that the churches will be able to overcome sexism and become instrumental in overcoming it. They can move from exclusive practices and beliefs to inclusive practices and beliefs, even if the implementation of these is still blocked by institutions that are uncomfortable with change. Change will be painful, but gifts and charisms of women cannot remain unwanted. The aspirations of women for equality in society and in churches will lead to painful encounters with the establishment forces and with the institutional churches. But these encounters will be necessary before the institutions will accept an atmosphere of trust. To let go, is to trust. To let go of old concepts, is to invest new ones with trust. Women are no longer strangers in the decision making processes, they are no longer subject to punishments if they hold different views, they are no longer 'much beloved daughters' who will keep silent in church. We, the women, who have come through the fundamental oppression of being viewed seductresses, therefore in need of control, we have learnt to turn the other cheek and accept God's all embracing love, not patriarchy's prescriptions. We have searched for the lost coin and found it, we discern alternative pathways that lead to the liberation of all.

Feminist theologians have created new images for speaking about and re-envisioning God. We have left the crisis of male monotheism behind us and started to cross borders, to break down demarcation lines of worship. We have analysed mechanisms by which the church hierarchies distanced themselves from women and eliminated their agenda, we are no longer somebody else's sacrifice, nor do we allow any discrimination to be termed 'hallowed' any longer. Ours is a vision of transformation in which being together becomes being. Women have moved out from the slot of voluntary helpers for others to responsible workers for themselves.

Feminist theology is one way to help patriarchal theology to grow out of sexism. The lesson we would like those committed to patriarchal power to learn is beautifully expressed in *The Mabinogion*, the texts of Welsh folklore. There we are told that true leaders are not those who exert power over others; the leaders are the truly strong ones who make themselves bridges and by so doing aid others to move on and make connections with new places as well as returning to known places with new insights.

We believe that Christianity and patriarchy are not inextricably linked for all times. Feminist theology will enhance Christianity and liberate it from patriarchy. We therefore place before Christianity the opportunity to embrace this vision that is springing from the hearts, minds and needs of women and men around the globe. Christianity has a history of change and a founding principle of representing the marginalized. With the rampant growth of advanced capitalism there is no time to think of self preservation; it is time to act radically in defence of Gods creation in all its diversity. The time is ripe.

Glossary

It is beyond the scope of this book to compile a comprehensive glossary of words used in feminist theology, but it is worthwhile dipping into them to gain insight into the world it hopes to create. We will use definitions from a variety of sources as well as our own definitions.

Alienation   Experiencing the world and oneself, passively and receptively.

Biophilic   Life-loving. Something sadly lacking in patriarchal theology.

Crone   Woman who is an example of strength, courage and wisdom (Daly 1987: 15).

Dunamis   One's innate divine power.

Empowerment   The claiming of one's own energy to act purposefully in the world. It is aided through mutual relation.

Erotic power   The assertion of the life force of women. The desire to be involved.

Fantasy   A key to creating feminist theology. It includes imagination, inspiration, inventiveness, flexibility, freedom and creativity.

Female/Male   The biological division of the species.

Feminine/ Masculine   Characterizations of behaviour along gender lines, limiting the type of behaviour that is viewed as accepted for the sexes.

Friendship   This is synonymous with right, mutual relationship. It calls us to justice since friends are those who most often face us with ourselves and push us on. For many women it is their friendship with other women that empowers them.

God/dess   The divine can be most personally felt among people struggling for right relations. God is our power in mutual relation by which we nurture ourselves and others to liberation. In this way God is both transcendent and immanent as the active source of our creative and liberating power (Heyward 1989: 189).

Godding	The process of connecting to the roots of who we really are. Moving towards our divine nature. We not only use this process for ourselves but for others and the world as we aid others, through mutual relation, to their own becoming.
Hag	Unlike Christian saints, a hag is alive and is travelling into feminist time and space; a radical being (Daly 1987: 15).
Interconnection	A method and a goal of feminism.
Justice	Mutuality makes itself visible through just actions and relations. Justice-making is our love-making in the world (Heyward 1989).
Machismo	The cluster of male traits related to masculine honour.
Mamismo	An attitude by which mothers are placed on pedestals by their sons who are in turn totally indulged by their mothers.
Mutuality	A dynamic situation in which people 'call forth' one another to be more fully themselves. It means being, changing and growing in relation to those who are changing and growing in relation to us (Heyward 1989: 185).
Paradise	Cosmic spinning; movement that is not containable (Daly 1987: 6).
Patriarchy	Seeing the world in dualism and through the hierarchical values that are created by it.
Patriarchal capitalism	This is corporate monopoly capitalism in which monopolizing the modes of production is the sole aim of the economic system. It is patriarchal because it perpetuates the patterns of male dominance in the realm of political economy (Heyward 1989: 163).
Power	The ability to make a difference. It is an energy. Feminist theology sees power-over as evil while it views mutual empowerment as the goal of spirituality. Women have a great deal of relational power and must learn again that this has divine origins. Power experienced as the energy to connect with others on behalf of whatever strengthens the fabric of life is good, erotic and relational. It is God's power (Heyward 1989: 192).
Relation	This is the core of it all—we are all in relation just by being born. The feminist struggle is to create right, just, mutual relation.
Sensuality	This is our embodied feeling. By allowing ourselves to feel in this concrete way we become passionate enough to seek change, to strive for justice.
Sexism	The systematic undervaluing and exclusion of one half of the human race on the grounds of sex.

Shalom	A vision of a mutually empowering future. It replaces the term kingdom because of the patriarchal connotations of such a term.
Sin/Evil	Anything that breaks our mutuality and creates hierarchy and division.
Spirituality	Imagining wholeness.
Womanism	The term originated with Alice Walker and refers to black feminism.
Yourself/Myself	You must fill in the blank but we are all engaged in this process of becoming with expectant joy; we accept it with the loving arms of friendship and we thank each other for the struggle of selfhood. It is a battle you and I wage for us all; for God/dess.

Bibliography

Amiel, B.
    1991   'Men and their Natural Sexuality on Trial', *The Times*, 10 December.
Andolsen, B., C. Gudorf and M. Pellauer
    1985   *Women's Consciousness: Women's Conscience* (New York: Harper & Row).
Armstrong, K.
    1986   *The Gospel According to Woman* (London: Pan).
Beauvoir, S. de
    1988   *The Second Sex* (London: Pan).
Boff, L.
    1980   *Jesus Christ Liberator* (London: SPCK).
Børreson, K.
    1995   *The Image of God: Models in Judeo-Christian Tradition* (Minneapolis: Fortress Press).
Borrowdale, A.
    1991   *Distorted Images: Christian Attitudes to Women, Men and Sex* (London: SPCK).
Boyce-Tillman, J., and J. Wootton
    1993   *Reflecting Praise* (London: Stainer & Bell).
Brock, R.
    1988   *Journey by Heart: A Christology of Erotic Power* (New York: Crossroad).
Brock, R., and S. Thistlethwaite
    1996   *Casting Stones: Prostitution and Liberation in Asia and the United States* (Minneapolis: Fortress Press).
Brown, P.
    1989   *The Body and Society: Men, Women and Sexual Renunciation in Early Christianity* (London: Faber & Faber).
Buckley, M.
    1978   *Pope John Sunday Missal: A Treasury of Catholic Spirituality* (Leigh on Sea: Kevin Mayhew).
Bunch, C.
    1987   *Passionate Politics* (New York: St Martin's Press).
Chicago, J.
    1979   *The Dinner Party: A Symbol of our Heritage* (New York: Doubleday).
Christ, C., and J. Plaskow (eds.)
    1979   *Womanspirit Rising* (San Francisco: Harper & Row).
    1989   *Weaving the Visions: New Patterns in Feminist Spirituality* (New York: Harper Collins).

Chung Hyun Kyung
    1991   *Struggle To Be the Sun Again* (London: SCM Press).
Cline, S.
    1994   *Women, Celibacy and Passion* (London: Optima).
Crossan, J.D.
    1992   *The Historical Jesus: The Life of a Mediterranean Jewish Peasant* (San Francisco: Harper).
Daly, M.
    1973   *Beyond God the Father* (Boston: Beacon Press).
    1984   *Pure Lust and Elemental Feminist Philosophy* (London: The Women's Press).
    1987   *Gyn/Ecology: The Metaethics of Radical Feminism* (London: The Women's Press).
Daly, M., and J. Caputi
    1988   *Websters' First Intergalactic Wickedary of the English Language* (London: The Women's Press).
Dowell, S., and L. Hurcombe
    1981   *Dispossessed Daughters of Eve: Faith and Feminism* (London: SCM Press).
Drewermann, E.
    1990   *Kleriker: Psychogramm eines Ideals* (Olten: Walter Verlag, 7th edn).
Ennen, E.
    1984   *Frauen im Mittelalter* (Munich: Beck).
Ervin-Tripp, S., and L. Mitchell-Kernan
    1977   *Child Discourse* (New York: Academic Press).
Fabella, V.
    1983   *Irruption of the Third World: Challenge to Theology* (Maryknoll, NY: Orbis Books).
Fiorenza, E. Schüssler
    1983   *In Memory of Her* (London: SCM Press).
Fox, S.
    1990   *The Medieval Woman: An Illuminated Book of Days* (London: Collins).
Gebara, I.
    1999   *Longing For Running Water: Ecofeminism and Liberation* (Minneapolis: Fortress Press).
Gerber, U.
    1987   *Die feministische Eroberung der Theologie* (Munich: Beck).
Gibellini, R.
    1987   *The Liberation Theology Debate* (London: SCM Press).
Gilligan, C.
    1982   *In a Different Voice: Psychological Theory and Women's Development* (Cambridge, MA: Harvard University Press).
Gilman, C.P.
    1923   *His Religion and Hers* (London: T.F. Unwin).
Gimbutas, M.
    1982   *The Goddesses and Gods of Old Europe 6500 to 3500 BC* (London: Thames & Hudson).
Gouges, O. de
    1791   *Declaration des droits de la femme et de la citoyenne* (Paris) (reprinted in H. Schröder [ed.], xxx [Aachen: ein-Fach-Verlag, 1995]).

Grant, J.
    1989   *White Women's Christ, Black Women's Jesus* (Atlanta: Scholars Press).
Greer, G.
    1999   *The Whole Woman* (London: Doubleday).
Gregorovius, F.
    1923   *Das Ghetto und die Juden in Rom* (reprinted in F. Schulman [ed.], *Wander-jahre in Italien* [Dresden: Wolfgang Jess Verlag (1853)]): 287-304.
Gutiérrez, G.
    1984   *We Drink from our own Wells* (London: SCM Press).
Halkes, C.I.M.
    1978   'Über die feministische Theologie zu einem neuen Menschenbild' (Doku-mentation, 25; Frankfurt: Evangelischer Pressedienst).
    1985   *Suchen was verloren ging: Beiträge zur feministischen Theologie* (Gütersloher Taschen-Bücher, 487; Gütersloh: Gütersloher Verlagshaus, Gerd Mohn).
    1991   *New Creation: Christian Feminism and the Renewal of the Earth* (London: SPCK).
Hampson, D.
    1990   *Theology and Feminism* (Oxford: Basil Blackwell).
Harnack, A.
    1957   *What is Christianity?* (New York: Harper).
Harrison, B.
    1985   *Making Connections: Essays in Feminist Social Ethics* (Boston: Beacon Press).
    1999   'Feminist Ethics and Post Modernism'. Keynote speech, American Academy of Religion, Ethics Section, 20 November (Boston: American Academy of Religion).
Hartland, J.
    1991   *Language and Thought* (Leicester: BPS).
Heyward, C.
    1982   *The Redemption of God: A Theology of Mutual Relation* (Washington, DC: University of America Press).
    1984   *Our Passion for Justice* (New York: Pilgrim Press).
    1989   *Touching our Strength: The Erotic as Power and the Love of God* (New York: Collins).
Home Office
    1999   'Living Without Fear' (London: Home Office Publications).
Hunt, M.
    1989   'Spiral not Schism: Women-Church as Church', *Religion and Intellectual Life* 7.1: 71-85 (85).
    1990   *Waterwheel* 3.2.
    1991   *Fierce Tenderness: A Feminist Theology of Friendship* (New York: Crossroad).
Illich, I.
    1983   *Gender* (London: Boyars).
Isherwood, L.
    1999   *Liberating Christ: Exploring the Christologies of Contemporary Liberation Move-ments* (Cleveland: Pilgrim Press).
Isherwood, L., and D. McEwan (eds.)
    1996   *An A-Z of Feminist Theology* (Sheffield: Sheffield Academic Press).

Isherwood, L., and E. Stuart
  1998   *Introducing Body Theology* (Sheffield: Sheffield Academic Press).
Kapuscinski, R.
  1986   *Shah of Shahs* (London: Picador).
Kumari, R.
  1988–89   'Female Sexuality and Bodily Functions in Hinduism' (Report to the
              Geneva Conference on Women, June 1985. Summary in *Connexions*, 23.
              Oakland, CA: Translation Service, 28).
Kwok, Pui-Lan
  2000   *Introducing Asian Feminist Theology* (Introductions in Feminist Theology, 4;
              Sheffield: Sheffield Academic Press).
Lakoff, R.
  1975   *Language and Women's Place* (New York: Longman).
Long, A.P.
  1992   *In a Chariot Drawn by Lions: The Search for the Female in Deity* (London:
              The Women's Press).
Lorde, A.
  1984   *Sister Outsider* (California: Crossing Press).
Luther, M.
  1933   *Kritische Gesamtausgabe*, III (Weimar: Briefwechsel).
Mack, B.
  1993   *The Lost Gospel, the Book of Q and Christian Origins* (Shaftesbury: Element).
Martyna, W.
  1986   'The Woman Question', in P. Mayers (ed.), *Sociology in Focus: Gender*
              (New York: Longman): 97-125.
McEwan, D.
  1987   'Bishop, Priest, Deacon: Three Functions, One Precondition', in
              D. Brewster, D. McEwan and K. Walsh (eds.), *Celibacy in Control*
              (London: Fedouloff): 15-31.
  1994   'Ich liebe nicht die Autoritat, ich liebe mit Autoritat. Die Voll-Macht der
              feministischen Theologie', in *Frauen und Macht: Dokumentation der 1.
              deutschen Frauensynode* (Frankfurt: Spener Verlagsbuchhandlung GmbH):
              41-48.
McEwan, D. (ed.)
  1991   *Women Experiencing Church: A Documentation of Alienation* (Leominster:
              Fowler Wright Books).
McFague, S.
  1993   *Super Natural Christians: How We Should Love Nature* (London, SCM
              Press).
McNamara, J.
  1985   *A New Song: Celibate Women in the First Three Christian Centuries* (New
              York: Harrington Park Press).
Metz, J.
  1969   *Theology of the World* (London: Burns & Oates).
Miles, R.
  1989   *The Women's History of the World* (London: Paladin).
Moltmann, J.
  1967   *Theology of Hope* (London: SCM Press).

Moltmann-Wendel, E.
1986   *A Land Flowing with Milk and Honey: Perspectives on Feminist Theology* (London: SCM Press).

Morley, J.
1988   *All Desires Known* (London: MOW/WIT).

Morton, N.
1985   *The Journey is Home* (Boston: Beacon Press).

Oakley, A.
1982   *Subject Women* (London: Fontana).

Oduyoye, M.
1986   'Reflections from a Third World Woman's Perspective', in *idem* (ed.), *Hearing and Knowing: Theological Reflections on Christianity in Africa* (Maryknoll, NY: Orbis Books): 83-93.

2001   *Introducing African Feminist Theology* (Sheffield: Sheffield Academic Press).

Ohanneson, J.
1980   *Woman, Survivor in the Church* (Minneapolis, MN: Winston Press).

Pagels, E.
1979   *The Gnostic Gospels* (London: Penguin Books).

Palazzini, P. (ed.)
1962   *Dictionary of Moral Theology* (London: Burns & Oates).

Pisan, C. de
1982   *The Book of the City of Ladies* (London: Pan [1402]).

Pittenger, N.
1979   *The Lure of Divine Love* (Edinburgh: T. & T. Clark).

Popper, K.
1979   *Objective Knowledge: An Evolutionary Approach* (Oxford: Clarendon Press).

Primavesi, A.
1991   *From Apocalypse to Genesis: Ecology, Feminism and Christianity* (Tunbridge: Burns & Oates).

Ranelagh, E.L.
1985   *Men and Women* (London: Quartet).

Ranke-Heinemann, U.
1990   *Eunuchs for Heaven: The Catholic Church and Sexuality* (London: André Deutsch).

Raymond, J.
1986   *A Passion for Friends* (Boston: Beacon Press).

Reeves-Sanday, P.
1981   *Female Power, Male Domination: On the Origins of Sexual Inequality* (Cambridge: Cambridge University Press).

Roper, L.
1991   *The Holy Household: Women and Morals in Reformation Augsburg* (Oxford: Clarendon Press).

Rosaldo, M.A., and L. Lamphere (eds.)
1974   *Women, Culture and Society* (Stanford, CA: Stanford University Press).

Rouser, E. (ed.)
1990   *From Division to Vision: Report on the Third General Assembly of the Ecumenical Forum of European Christian Women* (York: Witten).

Rowbotham, S.
    1976   *Hidden from History* (New York: Vintage Books).
Rudy, K.
    1997   *Sex and the Church: Gender, Homosexuality and the Transformation of Christian Ethics* (Boston: Beacon Press).
Ruether, R. Radford
    1983   *Sexism and God-talk: Towards Feminist Theology* (London: SCM Press).
    1987   'Feminist Theology', in J. Komanchak, M. Collins and D. Lane (eds.), *The New Dictionary of Theology* (Dublin: Gill & Macmillan): 113-20.
    1989   Catholic Women's Network, Annual Lecture, London, 14 July (unpublished).
    1991   'Women's Difference and Equal Rights in the Church', in A. Carr and E. Schüssler Fiorenza (eds.), *The Special Nature of Women?* (Concilium; London: SCM Press, 6th edn): 11-18.
    1996   *Women Healing Earth* (London: SCM Press).
    1997   'Created Second, Sinned First: Women, Redemption, and the Challenge of Christian Feminist Theology', *Conscience* 18.1: 71-80.
Russell, L.
    1974   *Human Liberation in a Feminist Perspective* (Philadelphia: Westminster Press).
St Hilda Community
    1993   *Women Included: A Book of Services and Prayers* (London: SPCK).
Saiving, V.
    1960   'The Human Situation: A Feminine View', *The Journal of Religion* (April); republished in Christ and Plaskow (eds.) 1979: 25-42.
Sawyer, B.
    1987   'Shield-maiden and Virgin: Female Chastity as a Threat against the Social Order' (talk at the Third Interdisciplinary International Conference of Women, Dublin, 7 July, unpublished).
Schipper, M.
    1991   *Source of All Evil: African Proverbs and Sayings on Women* (London: Allison & Busby).
Sölle, D.
    1982   'Vater, Macht und Barbarei: Feministische Anfragen an autoritäre Religion', in B. Brooten and N. Greinacher (eds.), *Frauen in der Männerkircher* (Munich: Kaiser Verlag).
    1984   'Gott ist das Allermitteilsamste. Alte und neue Mythen', *Radius* 3: 65-74
Spender, D.
    1982a   *Women of Ideas and What Men Have Done to Them* (London: RKP).
    1982b   *Invisible Women: The Schooling Scandal* (London: Chameleon Editorial Group).
Stanton, E.C.
    1985   *The Women's Bible: The Original Feminist Attack on the Bible* (repr. Edinburgh: Polygon Books [1898]).
Starhawk
    1982   *Dreaming the Dark* (Boston: Beacon Press).
    1988   *Magic, Sex and Politics* (Boston: Beacon Press).
Steinem, G.
    1984   *Outrageous Acts and Everyday Rebellions* (London: Fontana).

Storkey, E.
    1985   *What's Right with Feminism?* (London: SPCK).
Stuckey, J.H.
    1998   *Feminist Spirituality: An Introduction to Feminist Theology in Judaism, Christianity, Islam and Feminist Goddess Worship* (Toronto: Centre for Feminist Research, York University).
Swidler, L.
    1979   *Biblical Affirmation of Women* (Philadelphia: Westminster Press).
Thistlethwaite, S.B.
    1990   *Sex, Race and God* (London: Geoffrey Chapman).
Torjesen, K.J.
    1995   *When Women Were Priests: Women's Leadership in the Early Church and the Scandal of their Subordination in the Rise of Christianity* (San Francisco: Harper Collins).
Trible, P.
    1973   'Women in the Old Testament', in *The Interpreter's Dictionary of the Bible*, Supplementary Vol. (Nashville: Abingdon): 963-66.
    1978   *God and the Rhetoric of Sexuality* (Philadelphia: Fortress Press).
    1984   *Texts of Terror* (Philadelphia: Fortress Press).
Valerio, A.
    1991   *Cristianesimo al Femminile* (Napoli: M. d'Auria).
Walker, A.
    1983   *The Color Purple* (London: Women's Press).
Warner, M.
    1976   *Alone of all her Sex* (London: Weidenfeld & Nicolson).
Webster, A.
    1991   'Separatism is not a Sin for Feminist Theologians', *The Guardian* (28 January): 4.
Westermann, C.
    1974   *Creation* (London: SPCK).
Whitehead, A.N.
    1929   *Process and Reality* (New York: Macmillan).
    1938   *Modes of Thought* (Cambridge: Cambridge University Press).
Wijngaards, J.
    1986   *Did Christ Rule out Women Priests?* (Great Wakering: McCrimmon's).
Wire, A.C.
    1995   *The Corinthian Women Prophets: A Reconstruction through Paul's Rhetoric* (Minneapolis: Fortress Press, 1995).
Wollstonecraft, M.
    1992   *A Vindication of the Rights of Woman* (London: Penguin Books).
Wootton, J.
    2000   *Introducing a Feminist Theology of Worship* (Sheffield: Sheffield Academic Press).
Wren, B.
    1989   *What Language Shall I Borrow?* (London: SCM Press).
Young, P.D.
    1990   *Feminist Theology/Christian Theology: In Search of Method* (Minneapolis, MN: Fortress Press).

Index of Modern Authors